A Hundred Days (
By
Claire Suyen Grace

A Hundred Days of Gratitude

Claire Suyen Grace

Published by Suyen Talken-Sinclair, 2021.

A HUNDRED DAYS OF GRATITUDE

First edition. September 10, 2021.

Copyright © 2021 Claire Suyen Grace.

ISBN: 979-8201715885

Written by Claire Suyen Grace.

Table of Contents

Dedicated to all the many minutes of all the many days, each one an open opportunity to see the spaces between the leaves and to treasure them.

INTRODUCTION TO A HUNDRED DAYS OF GRATITUDE...

Back in 2019 I was inspired by my friend Jools' Days of Appreciation, and decided to set up a Facebook page titled "A hundred days of gratitude", like Garcia's Solitude but not, so to speak.

The idea was to recognise one thing every day for which I am grateful, and to share it, sometimes with an anecdote and sometimes without.

I hoped the idea would spread out through my friends like ripples on a pond since it is often easy to focus on our troubles and woes without remembering how they may be a Life Lesson, and also to overlook reasons to be grateful.

With that in mind I selected thirteen friends at random to join me-but hoped that everyone reading would start focusing on being full of Gratitude for the lives we have.

The hundred days was scheduled to end just before Christmas, a fitting conclusion I think, to a meditation that celebrates our good fortunes.

This book is the result of those musings, they are mine and mine alone, and i take full responsibility for the views expressed herein.

Namaste.

Recent Reviews from 2020 Vision- The Wisdom of Hindsight

The book definitely resonated in a positive way....... It touched and met my soul, which is a very rare thing for me. It also resonated with me as a woman and as a mother and in so many other ways. And I have enormous respect for the work you do to try and rescue animals....... I wanted to know more about you and the other people who do it. I hope we will meet one day once Australia opens its borders.

It will make an awesome movie.

Very powerful indeed and you write so beautifully! Both cathartic and powerful... an incredible story.

Loved the book! Well done you!

Your book resonates so strongly with me... I am sixty, and have an adult son at home who is struggling ... It touched and met my soul, which is a very rare thing for me... It resonated with me as a woman, and as a mother, and in so many other ways... I am taking the time to adsorb your words, and delighting in it.

I found the book deeply moving...a beautiful read. Thank you.

I am feeling emotionally exhausted from reading it ! I have laughed and cried, felt pangs of longing and desire and everything in between. It is fantastic... So many of those close your eyes and savour the moment....in this wonderful, beautiful book. Bravo.

A Hundred Days of Gratitude
Day 1- Being Fat

Because only people who can afford to buy the food they need or want have the luxury of being overweight.

I wrote this somewhat tongue in cheek, but then i began to think about it.

Fat is not always caused by overeating of course, sometimes there are medical considerations that impact upon gut health and adsorption. There are also a plethora of mental health issues that impact upon lives via addictive behaviour, and i recognise that.

Nonetheless, being able to have food to eat at all is a blessing, one often taken for granted in the world we live in.

Day 2- A Comfortable Bed to sleep in

A comfortable bed to sleep in....

When I was a child, I went to boarding school in Sussex; loved it. Living in Liberia I spent term time holidays with my grandmother most of the time.

She lived in a very rundown 17th Century Welsh farm-workers cottage- no mod cons- hot water came out of a kettle and heat from a tiny coal fire. The walls really were over two feet thick and in winter the damp made your bones cold.

I used to share a bed with Nana.

The beds were old with brass bedsteads and made from chain link. The mattresses were feather filled and extremely cumbersome to move- every morning Nana and I would have to lift, toss and pummel the mattress to separate the feathers back into shape, and every night Nana would fill old glass pop bottles with hot water and cover them with a sock to heat up the bed. The heat made the damp palpable.

Nowadays I don't need to do any of that before collapsing into bed. I just lie down, pull my duvet up and sleep. In the warm, dry place that is my room.

Others are not so lucky. Others sleep on pavements, in carparks, under bridges, in storm drains, in ditches.

At this time of year in the Northern Hemisphere the cold and damp of winter is increasing.

And some of those people, who were once children themselves, will die in the only places they can find to sleep in.

Day 3- Tweezermans

Tweezers... the one luxury I'd request on A Desert Island Discs!!

Such vanity.

Vanity in our appearance is a two edged societal sword.

Should we dress up? Should we dress down? Should we care about our appearance? Should we not?

Does it really matter how we appear to others? Should it matter?

People definitely make judgements around how we look- should we let that effect our well-being and influence our appearance?

Tweezers- would be lost without them! LOL

Day 4- Sunny Mornings

It's an amazing bright, sunny morning today in Brigadoon.

I've always had a deep connection with Apollo, the Sun God- not due to any mystical teachings but just because I started talking to Apollo years ago and was blessed with sunny days as a result! Now we're taught that we create our own vibrational reality, so I'm grateful if mine is a sunny one!

Several decades ago in South African, I was due to get married at the end of January- their mid summer. It rained every weekend for the weeks preceding the date- but on the last day of the month the sun shone all day.

People were amazed- I kept saying that it was sunny because I'd invited Apollo to my wedding, and he came.

Day 5- Modern Plumbing

Travel, it is said, broadens the mind.

Well, that's just as well since I've seen some pretty ignorant tourists in my time!

Travel exposes you to different cultures, different norms and mores, different values.

Those of us who have travelled in countries where water is scarce will be familiar with the joys and challenges of trying to stay balanced in a semi squat while desperately hoping your aim is better than the environmental odours that accompany outside hole in the ground toilets!! My worst was at a zoo in the Ukraine where one simply balanced on the edge of a precipice and aimed behind you over a ditch....

Travel opens one's eyes.

At that particular zoo, animals were bred and sold illegally to line the pockets of the manager.

The state of the bear pens was heart- breaking, as were the living conditions of all the animals.

Every morning an old man would appear to feed the bears- on a bucketful of porridge. Nothing else, nothing more.

You could be forgiven for asking yourself how a zoo keeper would tolerate animals being kept in such hellish conditions.

One afternoon he came to me and asked, through a translator, if I could help his wife. She had breast cancer and they could not afford any treatment.

His monthly wage was 150 hryvnia a month.

One hryvnia is equivalent to 0.032 GBP

Travel, it broadens the mind.

Day 6- Good friends... and the not so good ones.

We are all grateful for our good friends- the ones who go the extra mile, pull out all of the stops, ride to our rescue and soothe our wrinkled brows... but the not so good ones, are we grateful for those too?

The not so good friends- the ones who leave us stranded in the desert, the ones who never call, the ones who are so self-obsessed that they are completely oblivious to our pain, our hunger, our struggles. The friends who disappoint us. Are we grateful for those too?

Well, we should be.

Those are the friends who teach us the deepest Lessons- who hopefully teach us how to be better friends ourselves, teach us to become more self-reliant and less dependent upon the goodwill of others. For every close friend that pierces us to the bone with their lack of compassion, harsh words and air of smug superiority, say a prayer of gratitude, and promise yourself to be a better person than they are.

Day 7- Getting Home

2018 was quite a spectacular year for me where housing was concerned.

At the beginning of the year I was told the landlords had decided to sell the house I had rented for four years. Then an amazing offer presented itself to me and it WAS too good to be true- that resulted in me moving into my house and then being told I had to leave twenty-four hours later! LOTS of shedding took place then as I had nowhere to live and too much furniture.

The recycling Centre was thrilled and all my furniture had gone twenty four hours after it was taken there.

Then I spent two weeks in an AirBnB- financed largely by my now deceased friend George, even though he himself was in dire financial straits.

I was snowed in for five days with my dogs- sadly the friend looking after my cats didn't realise that cats escape and I lost one that has still not been found.

By March I had found a place in Branscombe which although perfect in that it allowed pets, was not so good as it also added to them! Froglets, mice, toads, and other furries came and went- as did the power, the heating, the water and my sense of repose. After four months I was told I'd have to move at the end of the six-month contract- so I started looking.

And looking. And looking....

It took me an extra couple of months before I eventually found a property that I felt happy with, much to my family's relief, and I moved in four days before Christmas, when I expected all of our family to arrive for the holiday season !!

Absolutely hilarious!!

And so now here I am.

In my own little piece of Paradise- as George C used to refer to Devon- or as I refer to it, Brigadoon.

I love living here, love sharing living here with my family and friends-

And, EVERYDAY, I thank my lucky stars as I turn the corner at the top of the descent into B, whichever route I use, and see the beautiful Devonshire countryside before me- sometimes with a glimpse of the sea.

Being here was worth all the hassle of moving all those times, worth all the having to let go of things, the waterlogged books, the sheer enormity of not knowing what lay ahead-

The only regret is my lost cat Bronwen- but hopefully miracles will happen and one day she'll be scanned and come home.

Day 8- Nana

Today is my Grandmother's birthday.

As a child I was lucky enough to spend many happy times with her, and she taught me many things and gave me many wisdoms... As an adult I was able to share my children with her, and so four generations of family were able to share time and space. That was a great gift, for all of us.

In time I learnt that even my wonderful Nana was flawed, with her own dark places, but true love accepts the demons and the angels, and finds a way to tread in between.

I learnt a great deal from my grandmother, and treasure her memory deeply.

Day 9- Grief

Grief... Sorrow is the price we pay when we lose what we have treasured.

At its most gentle, it comes softly, after a time of anticipation, holding relief cupped against our breast in the hands of guilt.

At the other end of the horizon lies a far more visceral emotion. It is the grief that screams as our hearts are torn jagged from their bony cages, as we thud to the ground, our knees scraped and bleeding on the shards of glass that house our passions, our hopes and dreams. Our places of peace and safety and joy.

Our screams are silent, our tears only salty stains on dried out parchment.

This is the grief of broken promises and of disappointment, the grief that drives all logic from our minds and leaves behind only anguish and despair.

It is a grief that feeds upon itself until we are either consumed and lost in the greyness of a life without meaning, or we find within ourselves a wish to cease weeping, and cross the great divide.

There is no logic to it, no right time, no moving on, there is only a moment, a tiny ember that suddenly catches the breeze and is flickered into light.

May we all find the strength to fan the flames.

Day 10- Rice Cookers-

Sometimes the easiest option can be the best solution.

Day 11 - My Children

Our children hold mirrors so that we might see.

As I grew up, I can't remember ever discussing the prospect of having children of my own. Nor was there an unwritten assumption that one day I would be a mother. I have no idea why, but it just wasn't something we talked about.

In fact, I never gave it much thought.

Never agonised over whether it was a good idea, bad idea, good timing or bad timing- what sort of mother I'd be or whether children had a place in my life.

In my normal almost carefree manner, I lived life and at some point found myself the mother of two children.

And I was so lucky!! I can't remember ever feeling exhausted, or depressed, or traumatised or exasperated - I know I lost patience a few times to my shame, but they were a joy and a wonder to have around.

Now they are parents themselves, but I still think of them as my children! LOL

When I look at them now, I remember the long line of people behind them, my parents, their grandparents, great grandparents.... dozens of individuals who have given some part of themselves to the collective DNA.

And I feel so lucky.

Lucky that I was chosen to share their journeys, and to share the world through their eyes.

Day 12- Sharing Food with Friends

My father once told me that if I knew how to cook I'd never starve.

In more ways than one, his words proved true.

Over the decades I've sometimes had to earn my living cooking- sometimes in commercial kitchens, sometimes in private ones, and sometimes in colleges teaching adults.

I was lucky in that my mother taught me the basics of Oriental cuisine, my grandmother showed me how to cook English meals, and my own natural curiosity filled in several countries inbetween!!

Now both my children have grown up to be amazing cooks in their own right- and they have the added bonus of their father's baking genes.

Day 13- Self Doubt

There are times in life when we take a stand, certain that we are right, that our reasoning is just and our motives pure.

And then there are the times when we question our actions, and our reasoning and wonder if our motives were completely fair.

And sometimes there are days when you realise that your way might not have been the best way-

THOSE are the days to be grateful for. Those are the days when we grow.

Day 14- Night Time

I'm lucky and live in a quiet rural village in Devon. After dark there is next to no ambient light, hardly any traffic, and next to nobody outside walking about.

I walk my hounds late at night.

Nighttime brings its own evocations- smells, sounds, shadows-especially in the country.

When it's warm and humid, the air is full of deep dusky aromas that stretch out from under the hedgerows and the layers of microscopic lifetimes that lie hidden there.

Owls screech in woodland, the sea crashes and rolls down the valley, crickets chirrup and toads burp, and the stars and planets stay quiet above while a breeze gathers clouds and ushers them elsewhere.

Nighttime. Quiet, serene, a world of beauty in the dark... how blessed am I in my bubble of Paradise away from inner city crimes and Man's inhumanity to itself.

Blessed indeed.

Day 15- Shoes

Walk a mile in another man's shoes is the saying, before you judge his steps.

Walk a mile barefoot and you will start to question your own.

Day 16- Expensive Soap

Quality soap is one of my extravagances. Scents are so evocative.

Research has shown that our sense of smell can take us back in memory more than any of our other four senses, and so is now being used as a therapeutic tool for those with Alzheimers.

Whenever I smell a coal fire I am whisked back in time to walks along the lanes near my grandmother's cottage. Brisk autumnal days when the air was verging on frosty, the brambles were laden with blackberries, the skies a silvern grey. I can see our breath forming in the air and hear tardy blackbirds singing one last song.

Soap, with its caresses of rose and jasmine, lilac and lavender, orange blossom and lemon, conjures up far more sunny memories.

Day 17- Cats

When I was little, I was allergic to cats, so my parents ensured that I never touched one. Then, one day when I was about six or seven a cat strolled up to me outside- I was playing doctors outside and making paste out of talcum powder and water-

And I picked it up and cuddled it. No reaction at all!

From that day to this Cats have been a part of me. Big cats, little cats, hairy Cats and smooth cats.

I've been lucky enough to have cuddled lions, leopards and ocelots-

And to know first-hand the bonds that are possible with our feline companions.

My current black cat Strider is as affectionate as any dog.

Were I living in my own property I would definitely become the cliché old woman surrounded by many purring people- in Tintagel I came close with ten Cats and an otter, but that's another post.

Day 18 – Starry Skies

I've seen some great night skies in my time-

The Northern Lights in Saskatchewan dancing in winter, a whooshing orange ball of fire flying low over the sands of Wadi Rum in Jordan, the legendary green flash as the sun dipped behind the curve of the horizon off the North Cornish coast, full moons at Stonehenge and Glastonbury Tor, and many nights in rural England when the sky is a black canvas bejewelled with sparkling points of light. The Milky Way a gentle brushstroke washing through the dots.

It gives pause to thought when we realise that for the most part the stars no longer exist/ that the light we see set out on its journey lifetimes ago and has long passed from whence it came.

Day 19- Photographs

I'm that person who has the family history preserved through photographs, going back over a hundred years to the early 1900's.

Through my grandmother's childhood and those of my parents, passing by mine and moving on into the lives of my children and now their children.

It's a wonderful gift.

I have shots of Baden Powell at Scout jamborees, Talken farmers combining in the Great Depression, Lord Mountbatten dancing with my mother, Louis Armstrong playing in Southern Africa, and then a rich tapestry of personal family travels and adventures.

Photographs capture our legacies, frozen moments in the spirals of our existence.

In our now current digital age, the majority have their smart phones crammed with photographic images- what does that tell us about our selves and our desire to hang on to moments that stir our hearts and souls?

Print some, frame them, put them into books or albums, savour the image, the light, the textures- and remember the moment that created a part of you.

Day 20- Employment

So today is payday, and like so many people in the country, the money comes in and before the morning has even started the majority of it goes out. And I'm one of the lucky ones NOT on minimum wage.

We lurch from one pay day to the next, struggling to keep our heads above the water.

It's about priorities of course.

With me, I choose to keep animals, and two veteran horses in particular when I don't own any land.

I don't own my house either, and choose not to live in a bedsit somewhere grubby.

Choices that keep me poor.

But choices all the same, and my own.

I am lucky- I have a job, one that I know changes the lives of children and their families in a positive way- I just wish it didn't come at such a high level of financial exhaustion.

A long time ago now I walked away from a life of material comfort in order to be true to myself-

Best day's work I ever did- but the price has been a high one.

So when anyone starts telling me they'd rather be elsewhere I always ask,

What price, Freedom?

Because there are times in life when blood has to be spilt in order for new beginnings to be born.

Day 21 – Motorways

Motorways- love them.

I drive many miles every month one way or another, and am truly grateful for our national road networks and the infrastructure that supports them.

Roads are such great metaphorical tools for our Life journeys.

Starting points, destinations, detours, rest stops, fast lanes, slow lanes, blind spots, signals, lack of signals, roundabouts, slip roads, road blocks, wrong turns, foggy conditions, the far off horizon.

BUT, the most important one of all is that WE are the driver, in the vehicle of OUR choice.

Day 22 – Tomatoes

Early this summer I purchased four teeny tomato plants from a neighbour for 20pence each.

I planted them in an old cat litter tray and left them outside...

This month I've harvested several pounds of tomatoes.

My grandson apparently loves tomatoes-

Happy Crazy Nana.

Day 23- Cinemas

Went to see Downton Abbey with my daughter tonight- most enjoyable

When I was around eleven to twelve my father used to take me to watch matinees of spaghetti westerns in Monrovia.

We'd go to an old rundown movie house called the Gabrielle and he'd buy me some bubble gum from one of the street vendors. It was a special treat to have that one to one time with him, and I still love Erico Morricone's haunting whistling theme music for The Good, the Bad and the Ugly...

Spaghetti Westerns are all about the eyes, the music, the black hats and the white. In them, villains are villains and the good guy always gets the girl- if there is one.

Real life is not nearly so transparent. The subtleties, duplicities, hypocrisies and vagaries of 1920's England as illustrated in Julian Fellowe's masterpiece doth make us all victims of our shared histories.

Day 24- Cultural Diversity

When my granddaughter moved up to primary school, it became apparent that the closest one with the best academic feedback did not have any early morning or after school facilities for children whose parents worked nine to five.

When my daughter asked why no such provision was made, the Headmistress replied that none of the families needed after school care for their children as the families all had mothers or aunts or grannies to do that for themselves.

The school is predominantly Asian in its ethnic base, and one could say that my granddaughter is their "token white person."

Apparently, children are not the detritus of the Nuclear family as much here as they are elsewhere.

Children in my home county of East Devon are not nearly so fortunate.

With a majority of white-Anglo-Saxon-Protestant families, I have recently heard of disturbing and appalling racial bullying going on in the upper reaches of what is known as one of the best secondary schools in the country.

Here, it is an accepted custom for the Sixth Formers to "roast" one another online, frequently aimed at students of mixed race. Comments about colour, odour and overall inferiority are commonplace.

The intensity of the racial slurring goes on in the classroom as well among students, with the ignorance displayed surpassed only by the arrogance that condones it.

The victims themselves stay silent, wishing only that their skins were white so that they could blend more easily into the pallid majority of their fellow students.

When I was a child, I was blessed by growing up in a cosmopolitan West African country. My parents had no racial biases whatsoever, and

I developed with a solid underpinning of confidence based in my own mix of nations.

As I once said to a fellow pupil at my English boarding school-

While your ancestors were hitting each other over the head with the jawbone of an ass, mine were painting on silk.

I am so grateful that my two grandchildren living in Bury will have easy access to multiple cultural strengths, and hope that my two living in the heart of Devonshire will be able to survive the prejudices inherent to rural southern England.

I have my jawbone brightly polished in case they need to fit in.

Day 25 – Belonging

It's one of my greatest gifts- being made to feel welcomed by my children and their partners.

In these troubled times however I find myself thinking about all the displaced souls, those who have nowhere to belong in, whether that be geographically or emotionally.

When we are gifted a sense of Belonging, take the time to share that with those less fortunate, and be kind.

Day 26 – Perspective

Earlier, my grandson was standing within inches of a television screen watching Pepper Pig. I asked him to come away from being so close as the view would be better if he stood further back. He's not quite two.

His five-year-old sister agreed with me and happily stood next to him to prove my point.

You can't see the whole picture if you're too close, she said.

Indeed, one can't.

Day 27 – Pet Sitters

When I lived in Cornwall, I used to bring in three people to cover what I did myself- horses, exotics and domestic animals.

Nowadays I'm grateful for the kind friends and neighbours who hold the fort for me when I drive North.

Day 28- Strider

I asked for a feral cat, one to keep an eye on the rodent families at the yard, and was soon told that they had one. He was a stray that had been fed for six years or so by an elderly lady who could no longer continue to do so, and had asked the CPL to trap him.

I went to where he was being held on a farm and happily agreed to foster him. That was about thirteen years ago...

So I'm not sure he was as old as they said.

Within the first twenty-four hours I realised that Strider's temperament was not feral- he just wanted to be loved and cuddled, so he joined us at home and my Beatrix Potter syndrome survived- I love mice, and rats! Lol

Strider has become my most affectionate cat- one that must sleep wherever I sleep, moving from one side to another as I turn, so that he is always face to face with me. He's a tapping cat- gently tapping my cheek to remind me that he wants cuddles too.

Strider has adapted totally to a household where other animals have come and gone- he's seen Cats and kittens, dogs and birds, even young rabbits, and welcomed them all.

He's a special familiar, and tonight, as I write this, he's saying goodbye.

Ironically, he leaves me just as I am about to welcome a new kitten to the fold, and I am positive that he waited for me to return home from my week with Justine before sloughing off his own mortal coil.

By morning he will be gone; I shall miss him deeply.

Day 29 – Connection

We all talk about connection-

With friends, with nature, with geography, with family- and we are all connected... to the good and the bad.

Connections anchor us, they also let us fly, they support us and set us free. Connections make us aware- of others and of ourselves.

And in that deepest connection within us, as we reach out to touch the Divine, we realise that we are all gods and goddesses, reeling in the terrifying freedom of freewill and the powers of Choice.

For the only connection that really matters is that which connects us to the Truth within ourselves, and through that, to the whole of existence.

Day 30- Change

Lots of talk about Change right now with a Full Moon approaching,,,

Change- the Tower crumbling so that new and better structures can be modelled from the rubble.

Change- the time of Birthing a new reality, a new paradigm, a new Us.

Change- walking towards a landscape where you feel at total peace.

Change- being able to offer more money than needed and receiving some back in return.

Change.

Every thirty years or so Saturn completes a journey around our sun, and astrologists refer to this as a Saturnal Return in our life cycle. It heralds opportunities to reboot our habits, our entrenched behaviours and to take a different path.

Thirty years...sixty, ninety.

Change.

If not now, when?

Day 31- Humour

British humour is a rare beast, it combines slapstick, bawdy, sarcasm, innuendo and most and best of all, irony.

It is often self-deprecating, since it's considered rude to blow one's own trumpet, although we guffaw loudly at lavatorial jests around gas and getting caught short.

Humour allows us the freedom to laugh, and sometimes to laugh and then catch ourselves in the spotlight of shame- how cruel are those videos of people being humiliated or worse, that their supposed loving friends and family share with the public, for example, and often- OMG- for money?!!

And then there's black humour- no, not racist comments made to belittle others, but humour that makes us laugh and then think about the grim reality behind the joke. Gallows humour.

We Brits are VERY good at that.

Tonight I wept.

I woke up at half past three and missed my cat Strider. I missed him lying beside me, sleeping between my arms, purring so loudly that the sound still hums in my brain.

Bailey was asleep on the bed, but in his own space of grief. He purrs but very softly, a quiet acknowledgement of content, but not the roaring assertion of delight that was Strider's trademark.

In those early hours, with a storm battling outside- wind chimes going crazy- I started thinking about Strider's last hours. The rectal bleeding,

padding under his tail to absorb the blood- very Virgo, very practical- the repeated vomiting, the convulsions, the spasms, and all the time, the purring.

I had him wrapped in a towel so that I could hold him in my arms, wipe away the dribble, stroke his head, whisper to him in the hope that somewhere deep inside his brain he could still hear me, feel my presence, know he was loved.

This morning I finally wept. Sobbed.

And then, there's that humour-

Took me six hours to bury the cat- he kept struggling.

Day 32 - - Horses

After reading the Navajo Song of Horses, how could I not be grateful?

Horses have been part of my being for decades. I wasn't one of those children blessed with a pony- living in Africa, moving, boarding school and cost, all prevented that. I did take riding lessons at school though, my mother happy to support my wishes, and on weekends I often walked the sixteen miles round trip to the stables and back in order to get an extra two hours in the saddle. I was thirteen at the time.

Horses. So many many stories, so many Lessons.

My very own horse was a gift from Hugh, an ex-racing Thoroughbred for £800 that looked like a black version of Rosinante in the worst cartoons.

I named him Saracen and he nailed my coffin shut tight around love, dedication, determination and resilience.

Aka responsible horsemanship.

Horses changed my life.

They were the reason I met Hugh.

They introduced me to people who became close friends for life, and opened up doors to adventure I'd never dreamed of.

They nourished my soul.

They taught me what values are important.

They still do.

Day 33 – Reflections

It occurred to me yesterday that people who look at us always see our left eye on their right. We are always seen as the mirror reflection of ourselves. It's a n entertainment to try and imagine what we would look like if what was seen was what is on the inside of our faces, left eyes on the left. And that started me thinking about reflections- reflecting on them, as it were.

Hamlet muses,

And the native hue of resolution is sicklied over by the pale cast of thought....

Act in haste, repent at leisure, etc etc, but as often found, every good proverb is contradicted by another equally good one-

Strike while the iron is hot! for example.

So, which to follow? More haste, less speed, or the early bird getting the worm?

We choose which sayings to apply, much as we choose our perceptions of the world around us.

These days, I find myself far more circumspect than I was twenty years ago- Life has taught me that a dripping tap can cause as much damage as a typhoon if you're an ant.

Day 34 – Music

Music...

I was brought up surrounded by the music of my parents- Nat King Cole, Fitzgerald, the Dean Martin rat pack- Sinatra, Sammy Davies Junior, then the opera...

Weekend curry parties that started on Friday and finished early Monday mornings. Our house at the top of two hundred and fifty foot cliffs above the crashing Atlantic. Three curries and at least two dozen side dishes. Maria Callas singing La Boheme or Tosca or any of the Puccini arias, belted our into the darkness at top volume into a black velvet tropical sky covered in stars. And listening, my father's best friend, his face awash with tears.

Day 35 – Dawn

I'm aware that I am one of the lucky ones. I awake to the sound of birds, awash with light that casts rainbow refractions around my room. The cat sleeps, the dogs snooze, and I'm warm under the duvet, safe and sound.

Not so everyone.

My working self knows about the deprivation and despair rife amongst our society's disempowered, and how that has come to be -both the disempowerment and my awareness of it- is far too long a story for this post.

Cast my eyes further afield to countries overseas and there are many who will not be as grateful to the dawn as I am- people living in terror, under oppression, people who hide in the dark to survive the cruelties of daytime.

And all we can do is try to make our own minute corner of this existence better, in whatever way we can, for whoever and whatever we can.

Dawn gives us that opportunity to have another go at doing so.

Day 36- Dessert

So, this evening a special friend came for dinner and arrived bearing many goodies!

Bramley apples, I stuffed them with bramble jelly and chopped Brazil nuts, topped with brown sugar and butter, melted chocolate over them before serving.

Deliciously wicked!

Thanks Tammy. Xxxx

Day 37 – Resolution

For a while I used to confuse entomology with etymology- the definitions that is.

Then I wanted to look at the word Resolve, and realised that I finally knew which was which.

Anyway, Resolve.

I wanted to use "resolution" as in the coming together of differing factors, as in agreement after debate, and then I thought, resolution as in the fining down of focus, the seeing of more detail, and then I thought, that is the same.

Is it? Then I looked it up.

I'm going to leave you to do that yourself, there are many meanings for the word I learnt, but I liked best its Latin roots-

To loosen and solve.

We all sometimes need to loosen our preconceptions, our judgement, our opinions, our knowingness, in order to seek a different path, and solve a situation we do not want to exist.

Resolution-

A Way of Peace.

Day 38 – Michael McIntyre

For making me laugh.

For observing the foibles of Humanity.

For sharing the humour in all things, especially when it comes within a mirror that illuminates our own need to rethink how we respond to others in our world.

Day 39 – Devonshire

For the leafy hedgerows, the winding lanes, the storm tossed shingle, the clear nights, the nut laden beeches and oaks and hazels, the blue skies, the clarity of light, the fresh fruit, the farm shops, the cry of gulls, the smells of fish, the moonlit moors, the tiny songbirds, the fields of sheep, the thatched cottages, the bustling city, the miles of open horizon to France, the valerian, the butterflies, the springs and rivers, the pasties, the clotted cream, the people.

Day 40- The smell of bacon cooking

Forty Days... wow... In the Wilderness comes to mind.

Bacon.

The smell of bacon cooking is one of the hardest things to ignore for vegetarians - most of my veggie friends admit to this, sighing deeply at the same time with wistful regret.

I was raised a meat eater, and as an adult who loves to cook and often earned my way by doing so, I confess to actually liking the taste of dead animals' body parts.

Nowadays however, I try not to eat them.

I'm not a purist- I don't stand on principle when invited to someone's house and it turns out to be a piece of meat- the Buddhists believe it churlish to refuse food when it is offered with love, and I agree with that.

Or am I simply copping out because I want a hit of animal protein? Sometimes I wonder, but at least I AM wondering.

This morning, tidying my patio garden, I smelt bacon.

And although the smell reminded me that I was hungry, and aren't pancakes with bacon and maple syrup just Divine?!- it also reminded me of some pigs I saw yesterday incarcerated in pens in a barn at a farm.

My reaction when I saw the pigs yesterday was one of deeply felt sorrow, and while I respect farmers work very hard to maintain their livelihoods, I can't help but wish they farmed a different crop.

So, today I didn't want to settle down to a meal of fried or grilled piggie pieces, today I was just sad that other people do.

And today, because of the smell of bacon, I am grateful that I have the awareness to recognise how the bacon reaches the plate, and that while I know how delicious it is, I have the strength, and the ability, to choose not to eat it.

Day 41 – Apples

Here in Brigadoon, apples are aplenty. It's been a bumper year for crops, and several people are putting out Bramleys at their gateways with signs asking passers-by to "Help yourselves."

It's a lovely gesture of generosity and kindness. Friends I know are also spreading the bounty, eager to give away bagfuls to whoever would like to have one.

So I started to think about apples, and their versatility and then I suddenly thought,

Why an Apple in the Garden of Eden? Why did the writer of Genesis decide that the Tree of Knowledge bore apples? Why not plums, or pears, or dates?? Why was the serpent up an apple tree?

And then, importantly, where do apples grow? Which climatic zone produces apples?

I'm not going to even start on the topic of who wrote the chapters that were bound together to create the King James Bible, or the history behind them, but the humble Apple obviously appeals to storytellers, luring both Eve and Snow White to the forbidden side.

For me, they delight my horses, are extremely versatile for eating and cooking, and have a whole host of homeopathic medicinal qualities, AND taste good.

So I'm grateful that a little thing like tempting Eve (let's face it, if the Snake had offered her a coconut would she have taken it? I mean, all that work needed to crack the damn thing! Or a lime? One bite into the skin and she'd have stopped right there, condemning Mankind to blissful ignorance forever!) has been long forgotten, and we can enjoy the fruits of the tree of knowledge with impunity...

And lots of double cream.

Day 42 – Indian Summer

Those wonderful warmer than expected days of mid to late Autumn...
when we can steal an hour or two in shirt-sleeves or picnic on the grass
or sit in the rays of a low-slung sun sipping cider.

Chances to be still and remember other warmer days.

Day 43 – Technology

Back in the Middle Ages when I was sitting my O level exams, calculators were just starting to come into vogue. There was huge controversy around whether or not students should be allowed to use them in exams, or whether the calculations should be done manually, or with a slide-rule. I had a slide-rule because I couldn't afford a calculator, and there was a quasi snootiness around not relying on technology to do your sums for you.

That was forty-five years ago, and technology had come a very long way since then. I have no idea what students do now...?!

I'm fascinated by technology- love it when it works- frustrates by it when its human operators screw it up.

Nowadays we are dancing around the ideas of automatic pilots, AI surgeons, and nanochips inserted into our brains to provide instant knowing.

I choose "knowing" because knowing is not the same as Knowledge.. or is it? I think of books- and how having War and Peace installed via nanochip might differ from the process of reading the actual book. My father used to argue why waste time calculating your twelve times tables when a calculator could tell you the answer much faster- do we need to know how to multiply numbers or is it just the result that matters?

I'm not certain about the sciences, but I'm pretty certain that with the Arts, knowledge is a process- a process that results from long, drawn out thought and internal debate. As we read a book, or study a painting, we think- hopefully!!- about what we are reading about, and those thoughts shape the way we feel, perceive, relate to the people and world around us. And that too changes with time, as we read or observe more.

Instant knowing has none of the nuance, subjectivity or abstractions that comes from the process of thinking.

So, technology. I love it. I use it daily. And then I think. Because I AM.

Cogno ergo sunt

OR

Cognito ergo sum?

That is the question.

<u>Day 44 – Shakespeare</u>

I've always loved the written word, and the writings of Shakespeare soon became a favourite of mine as I studied my way through them at various levels. O level English, grade 13, High School, undergrad introductions and finally Honours essays for my degree.

Shakespeare is either made or ruined by those who teach it. My father had a deep dislike for the Bard because the Brothers at his Marris school in Jo'burg used to rap his knuckles with a cane or worse if he couldn't recite Hamlet's soliloquies. Evil bastards some monks are.

Likewise some of the nuns at my mother's convent- frustrated spinsters full of their own power and moral indignation taking it out on young children.

An avenging God indeed, and no friend to the teachings of Christ.

Shakespeare's plays and sonnets buoyed up my views of the world as I journeyed through Hamlet's existential angst, questioned our perceptions and priorities, endured heartbreak and finally motherhood and unconditional love.

Thanks to Hollywood, Shakespeare has become more accessible, with that delightful Shakespeare in Love (you need to know your Shakespeare to fully appreciate the humour), and the more serious adaptations from Kenneth Branagh, when you do not.

Sonnet 116- Let me not to the marriage of true minds admit impediments

(Minds, not hearts or souls- discuss)

To Be or Not to Be....

Out, damned spot!!

And last,

Fie, fie! Unknit that threat'ning unkind brow!

We have the whole world held up for examination from a writer of five hundred years ago- the eternal Truths haven't changed a bit, and that is the big Lesson behind Shakespeare- that the motivations behind our behaviours are relatively constant, they are at our deepest core.

We need now to reacquaint ourselves with our souls and remove the centuries of dross that tarnish our highest potential.

The time, indeed, is always- and always means Now.

Day 45- Letters

My entire life has been blessed with letters- the written ones, often by hand or typed from my father and male friends. Letters and notes and cards-

All precious.

They are like the background webs of our lives. I have letters from my parents when they first fell in love under Caribbean skies, their letters of longing when my father sailed away into the sunset-

Literally- before my mother followed him.

Letters from my father to his parents when he went to boarding school, and later from when he crossed Africa on a bicycle.

Letters from my mother's father begging her not to leave Guyana and place her daughters in the care of their father.

Letters from my grandmother's great love, one sent every day for many years.

And then there are my letters- letters sent home from school, from university, from London, from years in Tintagel. My father kept them all.

I have love letters too- memories of souls now passed and on other adventures.

I have kept cards, full of love and sentiment, of longing and grief. Emotions captured and transferred onto paper.

Although more recently I have winnowed out the ones kept only for their visual beauty.

Letters.

I have the letters my mother wrote to me after my father died, the notes she included in my birthday and Christmas cards, her feelings and sadness laid bare upon the page, the immense loss still reaches out and grasps my hand.

And now, we don't do letters anymore.

We text, we email, we phone, maybe- usually though it's a few seconds of tapping and we're gone.

For myself, I like the actual physicality of writing- but my fellow writers have all gone. My parents, my grandmother, Francois- an amazing man who worked for the AFP and wrote remarkable letters- my friend Nancy, who no longer wants to connect, and my aunt Eunice, who is now no longer capable of writing.

I don't write letters anymore either- and as if they know, my fountain pens have all now broken in some way through age.

Letters capture moments and make them last forever, they preserve feelings and observations, thoughts and perceptions, and because they take time to create, reflect processes around those same things.

The webs of yesteryear have become the cobwebs of today.

Time to dust them off and make room for new gossamer ones instead.

Day 46- Language

I started off by thinking The Three R's...

Reading, Writing and Arithmetic, but was immediately amused by the non sequitur, so I started thinking about the English language itself.

English is one of the hardest languages for foreigners to understand, it's full of contractions, euphemism, colloquialisms, nuance, allusion and a whole snake pit of satire and irony inherent to the use of the language itself- just knowing vocabulary really doesn't cut it. Then there is the totally illogical spelling, a real minefield for students of linguistics, which is the cause for much frustration and disdain among users of social media!

Language is one of the primary means of communication- but English can so easily be misinterpreted. When written, the subtleties of tone that come from nuance are missing, hence the countless arguments caused by misunderstood text messages these days.

When spoken, words have to be carefully chosen so as not to give the wrong message- often possible in the heat of a moment.

I have a deep affection for words- for their usage, because I'm a firm believer that we all need to communicate with one another as deeply, honestly and as openly as is possible-

It is the way to further understanding, to find common ground and to create harmonious relationships.

So the next time someone criticises correct apostrophe use as being pedantic, just remember the panda and the cowboy-

Eats shoots and leaves.

Day 47 - Vision

When I was growing up, my friends and I would ask ourselves, which would you rather be-

Deaf, or blind?

I always chose deaf, because being able to see meant that I would be able to read- not just books, but instructions- typical Virgo- and so wouldn't be floundering about in the dark- literally or metaphorically!!!

And every day here in Paradise I feast my eyes on the natural beauty around me, I look at photos posted by loved ones, read reports for work, watch lives unfold around me, drink in the unspoken languages of animals, cast my eyes up into the heavens and drink it all in.

I still choose being able to see over being able to hear.

Vision though, is something else. The word implies wisdom, clarity of perception, altruism and awareness of truth.

And for vision, we don't need sight, we need only integrity, and the ability to hear all the noises within the silence around us.

Day 48 – Sundays

There is something special about Sunday, even if you're not working a nine to five. Maybe it's a centuries old awareness that the Sabbath was a day of rest- before people clamoured for seven days of commercial availability which was before the present age of ever available internet shopping.

Sundays at school meant Church, letter-writing, tidying drawers and a long afternoon walk up on the Downs after a roast lunch.

At home with my parents, Sunday mornings were the time for debate around the breakfast table- heated discussions between my parents and myself on a myriad of topics.

More recently, Sundays are a time of family reunions, when we share what has become a customised Sunday breakfast of American pancakes, smoked bacon and maple syrup.

It's the breakfast I also always serve my houseguests, if they eat bacon.

Sundays are also a time when I used to ring the bells- a skill I learnt just over thirty years ago while expecting Justine- poor child, bombarded in the womb by both crashing noise and the vibration of a tenor bell, Justine has no small antipathy for campanology.

Best of all though, Sunday is the day when we can all take a break- if we choose to- from the hustle and bustle of the weekly grind, the job, the school-run, the shopping, the chores, and just stop to enjoy the moments- whatever we use them for.

I know Sundays are no longer treated with the reverence once imposed by the Church, but we shouldn't lose sight of us all being a little bit divine, and as such, deserving of a special day of worship.

Because we're worth it.

Day 49- Cups of Tea

Sometimes tea just hits the spot. It's just the right temperature, the right strength, with the right amount of milk and maybe sugar. It's so good that you just want to swig it down almost burning your throat. And you always ask for a second one, hoping, just hoping, that it will be as great as the first

Tea drinking is an art form in the Far East, particularly in Japan, where women spend many years perfecting their Tea Ceremony.

While across the globe it symbolises a coming together in friendship.

These days we have many teas- black tea, green tea, white tea, fruit tea and herbal tea... tea served with or without milk, hot or cold, sweetened or not so.

My dear Pakistani friends make me tea in a saucepan, liberally mixed with evaporated milk and a handful of aromatic spices and sugar to produce what we think of as Chai Tea... tea Tea.

When I first arrived in England I was intrigued by people who put their milk in first- how did they know how much each person wanted? I soon realised that you accepted your cup regardless of whether you liked it or not in polite society. One wasn't there to enjoy the tea but more to fulfil a social function.

My grandmother taught me that when calling on someone for tea, you never took your leave before your cup had gone cold- very bad form indeed.

Tea in England has become a cultural reference point, an icon that foreigners immediately recognise.

And here it is a way to bridge gaps, mute awkward moments, show affection and add a touch of warmth to an otherwise grey day.

When my son was growing up, he would use tea as an olive branch, the weightiness of an apology sometimes too onerous.

The words, "Do you want tea?" were a way to break down a wall, to make a gesture of resolution, to change gears into a more reconciliatory pace.

I always said "Yes please."

Day 50- High Places

I'm a percher- that person who climbs as high as I can go and then likes to sit with my legs dangling over a precipice as I look out over a wide expanse. It doesn't have to be mountains and cliff tops, sky risers and planes will do too. I think I was an eagle in a previous life.

Thinking about my love of heights started me off though on why do we associate going upwards as being better than going downwards? Why do we think heaven is above us and hell below- why do so many of our myths and legends across time and civilisations have us going up into the Light and down into the Darkness and Doom?

So there I am on the top of the mountain, the fulcrum by its very design of my journey.

But I don't stay there, do I, I come back down from the summit, come back down the mountain and complete the journey.

As do we all.

Life must be about climbing our mountains, experiencing that uphill journey to reach a place where we can look out over all the obstacles beneath and behind us, take time to adsorb what we have learnt, before beginning the journey home with new awareness and new knowledge. And we go down to do that.

It made me realise that it is not Enlightenment that is the goal, but rather the integration of that enlightenment into our everyday lives, because even the Eagle comes home to roost.

Day 51- Emery Boards

My mother had nails to die for- real Chinese Empress nails, and always beautifully manicured. My father always carried a small nail file in his wallet, and to this day i like to see a man with clean nails. Mine are also long, grow quickly- takes six weeks to grow in a full set from a short trim LOL- and emery boards are my weapon of choice. A long time ago i read that emery boards are better for your nails than metal files.... Virgo.

I used to bite them, until one Lent I decided to stop. So I did. Virgo again.

Emery boards smooth edges, remove the rough bits that cause irritation- for me, they rate right up there with tweezers on my desert island.

Day 52- Colour

Black and white photography is different to a coloured palette- the lack of colour concentrates the mind on textures and shapes, while coloured images work on an entirely different level.

Our lives are full of colour- and thanks to the cone shaped receptors on our retinas, we observe all the subtle variations of our rainbow.

Colour distracts us. It fills our visions with joy and light-heartedness, its absence throws our reality into a completely different spectrum.

Literally and metaphorically, our existence is impacted by the colours around us, those we perceive and those that we create.

Today I wanted to say Orange, but it goes much deeper than just a colour, it goes to the very roots of the connections we make to certain colours- and the million dollar question must be-Who knows if what you see as a colour is what I see when I think of the same word...?!

Perception - colour- sight-

Black and White- only simpler until you start to think about it.

Day 53- Kindness

Every day we are witness to countless moments of kindness, from people who cross our paths total strangers to those family and friends that provide us with love and support.

And we too are kind, and to be given the opportunities to be kind is a real gift. It gives us an opportunity to behave with grace, and compassion.

Sometimes kindness comes dressed in less recognisable clothing- it comes as the unsought advice, the assertive challenge, the immovable barrier- it is this kindness that wakes us up, slaps us across the face, wakes us up to other possibilities.

We are always grateful for the first type of kindness, perhaps less so for the second. The second however should be seen as a kindness that cares enough to risk derision, alienation and rejection. It is a kindness prepared to risk itself in order to preserve the wellbeing of another, and that IS the definition of being kind.

Day 54 – Expertise

And being able to use it to help others.

I've been very lucky, all my life there have been remarkable individuals near to me that have been willing to freely share their knowledge and wisdom.

And sometimes I'm in the privileged position of being able to share that know how, to people who are receptive and welcoming.

That really does bring deep joy.

Other times I am aware that certain knowledge or awareness may not be welcome.

At those times I find it best to become silent and simply live my own truth.

Genuine ignorance, as in not knowing, cannot be helped, as it often reflects a scarcity of exposure or education- and I'm not talking schools here.

Chosen ignorance, as in truly not wanting to be more aware, is often based in fear or ego, and is far more difficult to enlighten.

I've been very fortunate, having had great teachers- of all kinds- from the day of my birth.

I endeavour to share that bounty whenever I can.

I am not always successful.

Day 55- Hay

Affordable, clean, non-dusty hay that's delivered.
  Every horse owner will know exactly how happy that makes us.

Day 56- Rainbows

There is something magical about a rainbow, to look up to the sky and see an arc of different colours leaping through the heavens. These days, rainbows are frequently seen attached to the manes and faces of unicorns, since as every parent knows, that's where unicorns reside.

The rainbow is also the sign of God's covenant with Noah after the flood, when God gives to mankind his promise that never again will he send water to destroy Man's dominion upon the Earth.

And rainbows are behind the myth of the Native Indian legend, where Warriors of the Rainbow will rise to create a world of justice, peace and freedom for all mankind- the truth behind the myth is far less inspiring and certainly far less ancient according to researchers, but the myth has become part of our global consciousness.

Like Genesis.

Ironic really.

This afternoon, driving along the motorway. an entire rainbow curved beside me, the light resulting in one end seemingly resting somewhere beside my car window as I moved at speed, it was a delightful delusion, full of magic and wishes.

A few months ago, one of my granddaughters in a rare show of angst spat at me,

I can't dream about unicorns ALL the time!

Although the next morning she told me she had.

None of us can dream about unicorns all the time. None of us can conjure up rainbows to ride beside all of the time either. Yet we still revel in their simple beauty, feel them to be a part of the Divine mystery and promise of a better world.

We still dare to hope that after a storm light will shine through and create a wonderful show of colour in a previously dark sky.

Rainbows are magical.

Unicorns are to be found therein. Namaste.

Day 57- Bicarbonate of Soda

There are many household uses for bicarbonate of soda as we call it here in the UK, but what many people may not know is that sometimes too much stomach acid feels like a heart problem- hence the term

"Heartburn" I'm guessing.

Four times in my life I've felt it. The first and second time I just wondered what the hell was going on. The third time I really thought I was having a heart attack, which made me do some research and discover I wasn't.

The fourth time I made myself a drink with bicarb in water, the relief of symptoms- intense sharp pain- was almost immediate. Such a simple thing. Everything is easy when you know how to do it. Namaste.

Day 58- Irritation

For me, it's one of my dogs that's starting to lose her marbles and goes into Automatic Barking Mode.

Regardless of how many times I tell her to stop, she goes on, and on, and on, and on, and- you get the idea. She's a tiny dog and her bark has evolved into a sort of raspy smoker's cough- a hacking relentless smoker's cough that simply doesn't stop unless distracted.

I've found throwing her out of a high window helps.

Obviously not what I do, but I'd like to!

MJ is a source of constant irritation, the splinter under my skin, more so because everyone just loves her (she's tiny and cute and blah blah blah) but no one has ever wanted to free me of her- and Jack Russell's have NEVER been my breed of choice. But I bred her so I'm responsible for her, fourteen years and now with pancreatitis, failing eyesight and I'm bloody certain senility setting in. Or is that me??!

She irritates the hell out of me at times, in her small determined JRT way, pulling to go one way when I really don't want her to end up under that car (so much paperwork!), snuffling under ALL the furniture because she's certain there must be a small furry thing hiding under the bookcase- well, in my house there might well be if it weren't that the bookcase rests flush with the floor- and, barking. Again. Just because she can.

Irritating.

It makes me realise that if I, with all my education, grounded awareness, understanding and feeling, can be irritated by a small helpless animal in the twilight of her years, and want to wrap her muzzle in cello tape- I did that once many many years ago to a friend's cocker spaniel to prevent me going insane- it's hardly surprising that individuals with less self-control react inappropriately in their moments of stress.

I'm one of the lucky ones, I have the ability to step back and survey what is upsetting my equilibrium and to curb what might be an irrational and out of proportion response.

Not everyone is that circumspect, not everyone has the ability to be within the circle and simultaneously outside the circle looking in.

Feeling irritated reminds me that we are all human, that we all have irrational, emotional responses, and sometimes those responses far outweigh the stimuli for them. It reminds me to be patient, to question not just my own motives but also the reasons behind the actions of others.

It reminds me that however knowing we think we might be, everyone has an Achilles Heel, and we need to wear therapeutic shoes.

Sometimes the dog chews them.

Day 59- Trees

So many wonderful things about trees, so many wonderful trees!

The pictures in the gnarled bark of old oaks, the gaps of sky between the leaves of summertime canopies, the blaze of colours in northern hemisphere autumns, the giant buttresses of equatorial giants, the curative powers of the gentle willow, the white canoes of birch, the strength, the shelter, the beauty. The connection of earth to sky. The sheer enormity of Time.

Day 60- Ageing

With Day 60 comes the numerical reminder that it wasn't all that long ago that I turned sixty years of age.

It was a fabulous evening, enjoyed with my family and friends.

Getting older means totally different things to the two sides of my ancestry- for the Chinese, age is to be venerated, respected, admired and comes with a degree of serenity and acceptance- and seniority!

Not so my western counterpart. My friends have themselves said to me-

Something happens at sixty, you give up.

I'm sixty now, what's the point of trying to change?

You're thinking like a young person, but because you're sixty, your feelings must be real and not some idealistic dream.

When you get old you have to be more careful.

When you get old you can't do what you want to do.

When you get old you have to be sensible.

When you get old........

Ad nauseam.

Today at a birthday tea for an octogenarian plus six years, I listened as her friends- no spring chickens themselves- commiserated about how awful it was for her to be in the state she is medically.... by the end of which I thought, OMG, shoot me now!

I didn't say that of course, although I did point out the cultural differences in the way Age is approached here and in the East.

Old age in the UK seems to be open season on complaining, moaning, bitching, and basically making excuses for not doing the things we want to do- And that's exhausting- no wonder people feel "old", it's almost socially irresponsible to feel or act any other way.

Age implies experience, experience implies the opportunities for learning, learning implies knowledge, and if we are lucky, with knowledge comes wisdom.

We should all be clamouring to have as much time as possible in order to seek as much wisdom as we can find...

Age, old age, can really be a blessing.

All we have to do is stop fighting it, and "get busy living" it.

Ride the damn horse!

Day 61 - Laughter

Saturday morning I woke up to see my timeline full of things that made me laugh-

What a fabulous way to start the day!!

Day 62- Hot Water

I'm a shower person myself, and can truthfully say that I haven't bathed for months, LOL. I love the feeling of running water, and at this time of year, a hot shower to wake me up early is very welcome. My grandmother loved to bathe.

Back in the late 1960's/70's living in the unmodernised 17th C cottage, there was no such thing as running hot and cold water- there wasn't even a bath. Hot water was obtained by boiling a kettle, and washing one's body was a cold, frenzied business in winter over a Belfast sink in the kitchen. Washing clothes was a slow, laborious back-breaking chore bent over the sink with a wooden wash board.

Not even fifty years ago.

When Nana collected me in London from Heathrow we would stay overnight at a small hotel in West Kensington. In those days en-suite bathrooms were hardly to be found except at the top end of the market, and most hotels had communal bathrooms on every or every other floor for the guests to share.

Nana always had a bath that first night. She liked the water so hot that I think had an unsuspecting crustacean ever fallen into it, the poor creature would have been served up later with hollandaise and a cold Sancerre!!

Nana would lie in the bath and luxuriate in the heat, topping up the water every so often. I know this because we had to share the bath-time and the bath- water, guests were only allowed water for one bath so that everyone could have one.

Fifty years ago.

Hot water.

Today we turn a tap and hot water splurges forth- if we are fortunate enough to be able to afford the oil or gas or electricity needed to heat it.

Last year I spent the best part of six weeks without a means to heat water, other than my kettle. For that matter, we couldn't heat anything, and ice was on the ground outside and on the glass inside.

Took me back.

When I looked up the origin of the phrase "hot water" I was intrigued to see that it's credited with originating in the 1500's and although the consensus is that it means to be in trouble, the ideas behind the source of that trouble differ.

Cannibals putting people into pots, criminals having their arms submerged to ascertain guilt or innocence, the cooking of creatures....

And the phrase used to be, "it COST me hot water" which I found intriguing. Was the cost of heating water reflected in its worth, so that being in trouble, in hot water, meant that one had sacrificed a part of one's wealth- and then later, was "in hot water"?

For me hot water is a real blessing, whether for showers, washing dishes, cleaning floors or making tea! But it is curious that such a luxury has become synonymous with having a problem, being in trouble and possibly in great danger.

Two horns on the same goat- as with so much of our experience, we choose which one we hold on to.

Today is the 11th of November....

It's a good day to think about hot water and all its meanings.

Day 63- Pause

One of my closest friends said to me recently, "There are some days when I think: she's struggling to find something today."

Which made me start thinking.

Thing is, every day there is so much to be grateful for, but it's so commonplace, so ordinary- I'm grateful every day for water, electricity, my car- petrol IN my car!!- good roads, SatNav. the internet, Netflix, food, and so the list goes on.

I'm also grateful for those unexpected moments of pleasure, the sudden twists and turns of surprise, the quiet contemplations and the frenzied sprints.

And I'm grateful that I'm able to BE grateful, that I have the luxury of thought, the ability to ponder, the gift of philosophy...

Today it was unravelling a long length of electric cord. I'd moved the horses temporarily and needed to dissuade them from going walk about . No matter how well I think I've coiled old electric tape, it always seems to entangle itself with fresh enthusiasm when needed again months later. So I stood in the school, quietly trying to work out which piece of cord should be pulled, or twisted, or threaded through next. And I have learnt that the process is easier if you don't treat it as a linear one. Holding on to one end and pulling just doesn't work. You have to let an end go sometimes, find another place and start teasing the strands apart there. Sometimes you end up with several separate lengths of tape all untangled but still the whole piece is twisted into knots- and then, for no apparent reason, all the untangled bits join up and you have a clear run of tape.

Life can be like that too.

Sometimes you have to work simultaneously at different parts of a problem in order to be given the solution.

Sometimes you have to stop, pause and then just start one small piece at a time, knowing that if you just keep persevering, eventually the answer will present itself and you can move on.

And once you've moved on, you can pause, breathe deeply and seek out the next mountain ahead of you.

Day 64 – Demisters

So today, with heavy rain and near freezing temperatures outside, driving without working heaters and demisters has been quite the challenge. The windscreen glass is fairly old too, and so I'm guessing pitted in ways my eyes can't register but which prohibits me being able to wipe the glass crystal clear. It's quite the irritation.

I like to be able to see where I'm going when I'm driving. Now I know that some drivers happily cruise along with a heavy fog on their windscreens, hardly bothered by their compromised visuals, but I've never been one of them. So driving on a dual carriageway and looking ahead of me through a blurred focus really isn't my favourite rite of passage. Thank goodness it was still daylight!

Demisters are pretty much taken for granted by drivers- unless they don't work and you can't rely on what you see ahead of you. That results in a feeling of discomfort, dis-ease, as you wonder how best to negotiate the road ahead of you safely and to your best advantage.

And in life, there are some people who perform the same function. When things get hazy, foggy and misty, they send a focused energy to melt away the doubt, to make things clearer, to help make our life journey easier, safer and more enjoyable.

Those people are beyond value.

They are the demisters in our lives when we can't quite see the way clearly ahead, and all the usual buttons simply don't work.

Day 65- Less

My timeline is blessed with posts from several New Age thinkers, Light Workers, Energy Gurus and the like, so there is always a plethora of great positivity for me to adsorb.

Many of us are aware of the call to arms for a new Way of Being that is circulating in our world at these times...

And one of the ones we see often is that we should all be asking for abundance, for "more" of the things we want in our lives.

And therein lies the rub. The conundrum.

Energy Workers tell us that if we focus on the "lack" of something in our lives, we make that lack our reality. So, for instance, if we make a mantra out of "I want more money", we will be wanting more money all the time, and never have enough.

Thinking about this I realised that our culture concentrated around the "more is better" principle- the desire to HAVE MORE- as opposed to having Less. The culture of acquisition, of advancement, of financial profit.

And then the answer came, we shouldn't be asking for More, we need to ask for Less-

Less debt.

Less loneliness.

Less hardship.

Less difficulty.

Less whatever you want less of, and in that way we create THAT energetic reality.

And so Less really does become More.

Day 66- Hymns

Glorious morning today- walking the dogs in the crisp Autumnal air and in the sunlight brought to mind Morning hath Broken- made more famous of course by Cat Stephens that was.

Jerusalem was my mother's favourite, and as it turned out, my old school song.

"Bring me my bow, of burning gold-
Bring me my arrows of desire!"

Rousing words full of passion and intent.

I'm not so sure that younger generations would know what I'm talking about these days, if I started talking about hymns by name, or hummed the tune from the old Ancient and Modern hymn book...

Things change.

It's hard enough to get a congregation to sing Christmas carols, and church services are embarrassingly quiet when the organ leads in to a hymn.

Watching a series on Netflix, I've been impressed by the scale and enthusiasm and sheer power of the singing in some Evangelical American Churches. Such JOY!

We may like to look down our Anglican aquiline noses at the "happy, clappy" congregations, but their joy, love and passion in the name of the Lord can't be denied, and is definitely more people friendly than the cold, austere, self-flagellating psyche of the catholic (small C) church.

Hymns used to be a call to worship, a way of connecting Everyman to the Divine. And on a sunlit morning, surrounded by trees on a quiet hill, it's hardly surprising that one's heart is stirred into song.

Just as well only my dogs could hear.

Day 67 - Imodium

Now I KNOW you are thinking, TMI- too much information!!

BUT I recently learned how efficacious Imodium is for dogs with loose tummies.

A couple of weeks ago all three of my hounds succumbed with varying degrees of severity to some tummy upset.

Imodium helped.

SO grateful.

Day 68- Beatrix Potter

I asked my granddaughter whether she'd like me to read her a story- and she chose Peter Rabbit.

I love all of the Beatrix Potter books, and frequently refer to myself as a sufferer of Beatrix Potter Syndrome- by which I mean that I have a soft spot for rodents, ALL of them.

I was thinking about that this morning as I watched a juvenile rat scampering along my patio trellis to help himself to some bird food (some birds can't eat hanging on and so need their food flat on a surface) before scampering back home.

I've warned the rats a few times that they should stick to nocturnal forays as some people won't like seeing them, but the heavy rains have driven them uphill from their riverside homes and so every now and then they appear.

Rats have terrible press. Bubonic plague is hardly commonplace nowadays but people still equate rats with disease and underground sewage.

Maybe it's the bald tails.

So I started wondering what natural predators preyed on rats, and was genuinely surprised by the list- birds of prey, weasels, big cats and owls... No wonder they don't want to eat at night.

At university a pal of mine rescued his lab rat once the experimentation was over and wore her draped around his neck for years. She had holes in her ears from the electrodes.

Maybe she helped find a treatment for cancer- we'd never know.

A few years ago when I first moved to Devon, I was on a yard with the biggest, grumpiest Tom cat ever- and the photo that I didn't capture was him eating his breakfast from one side of a tub lid while a large rat shared it from the other side.

When I deep littered my horses over winter, I'd have whole families of little brown furry people gazing up at me from around the edges some mornings- some very very tiny, their black eyes twinkling and their whiskers twitching while their larger siblings went foraging. Beatrix Potter syndrome.

This morning, Bailey, my magnificent ginger and white feline, was eating his breakfast when he looked through the bedroom window and espied the young rodent on the picnic table. Bailey immediately went out and waited poised by the picnic table, looking upwards in anticipation.

Young Master Rat was oblivious, far too involved with eating the crushed up fat ball.

Bailey poised himself- all 6.5 kgs- and leapt, tapping Master Rat on the head. Rat squeaked in surprise and alarm before hightailing it quickly back through the honeysuckle and into the garden bank.

I had to laugh. Bailey was quite unconcerned at the sudden abandonment and curled up in the sunshine to listen to the birds.

Beatrix Potter syndrome.

Another generation awaits- I'm going to enjoy it.

Day 69- Autonomy

Autonomy...

I know what I believe the word to mean, but I looked it up anyway.
And the definition stated more than one meaning-
Self- governing
Self-directing freedom
And then, from Kantian philosophy,
The capacity to act with objective morality, rather than under the influence of one's desires.

And that one pulled me up short. Suppose our desire IS to have objective morality? It's not a definition of autonomy I had ever been aware of.

For me, the freedom to be self-governing is a real gift. In work, in my private life, I have an extraordinary amount of freedom, and I treasure it- I can walk my hounds at midnight and write on social media when the outside world is asleep.

That freedom comes at a price of course, freedoms always do, and mine is living on my own, not having to answer to anyone under the same roof, but not having anyone there to help maintain it either. My choice, my roof.

Back to Kant.

To do the Right Thing (who decides that? Society? And who teaches Society their morals? The Church? The State? We are no longer enthralled by either- we have become a society without steering or rudder in many ways) and not to do that which we might desire when that desire is at odds with objective morality....

Doesn't sound like autonomy to me, it's almost contradictory, as it negates self-governance and moves responsibility to the collective objective.

No wonder it's called Kantian philosophy.

My father would sometimes send me his musings after a glass or few of wine, often written in the wee hours while my mother slept.

He wrote once about whether the gnu ever contemplated its own death, as it grazed beneath the hot African sun, and whether it made any difference to its death when the leopard pounced why the leopard had done so.

It is my conviction that we are all ultimately responsible for our actions- I know the psychologists live to excuse us and point out why this isn't so- and I know all the psyche 101 stuff too- but at some point we have to claim our Selves back into existence, regardless of how frightening it is to do so, and own our lives.

Because only then can we have true autonomy- Kantian or otherwise.

Day 70- Art

These days, thanks to internet search engines, we can access all types of images from the world around us, dating from the very first cave paintings to contemporary sculpture. I often am delighted by the artwork which accompanies so much of social media threads, and impressed by the high quality of so many commercially unknown artists.

Art offers all of us a window into another perspective. Whether it is painting, music, sculpture or writing, art is an artistic interpretation unique to its creator, and as such, expands our own consciousness as we link into it. The effort of understanding where that link connects to us is what fascinates me.

My own connection with art began as soon as I could put paint on paper as a child, and developed more when as an eight year old I was gifted a great collection of oils, brushes, canvases and other artist paraphernalia by an eccentric Greek architect called Yannis Democopoulis. He weighed well over four hundred pounds, ran with a pack of wolves, and used to drink beer while eating raw chilies. Childhood memories are the best.

My father painted. Large four foot square or bigger on anything he could use- I remember his delight when he was first able to order by post from the States pure colour pigments. And to this day I treasure his praise about a watercolour fish I painted in Chinese style.

You've got it, Su, you've got it.

Childhood memories are the best.

Since then I've dabbled in several mediums- pen and inks, pencil, oils, acrylics. Occasionally I sell them. A string of my bow I've hardly drawn. Ha ha.

Art is all around us of course, we only need the eyes to see it, our hearts to welcome it and for our soul to welcome it in.

Day 71- Seagulls

The sound of seagulls in the morning, as you lie in bed with the sun streaming in- for many of us a reminder of how close we are to the sea.

These days seagulls have migrated away from the coastal towns and I used to see them flying in that hybrid orange light of towns at night when I lived further inland.

Always opportunists, seagulls have become unwelcome in many seaside resorts, where they swoop down upon unsuspecting tourists and take pasties and ice-creams literally snatched from their hands and lips. So much so that town councils are systematically killing them off and think of them as vermin, and locals often do far worse.

Seagulls once upon a time lived on the sea, a welcome sight for sailors adrift as it meant land was near. They followed the fishing boats and circled above calling as the catch waste was returned to the sea. Seagulls learnt to follow the farmers at ploughing time too, helping themselves to the invertebrates as the shears cut through the earth.

Images of a different time, before they could feast at rubbish sites and waste bins, full to overflowing with the detritus of the holiday trade.

I've rescued and reared a few over the years- sometimes teaching the young ones how to fly or the sick ones how to swim again.

Macawber was one such.

He was standing on the shingle next to the promenade showing no interest in our fish and chips, so I knew he wasn't well.

A young boy stood near to him looking worried and assured me that his parents had called the rspca who had promised to be there in twenty minutes. I assured him- and his parents that the rspca definitely would NOT be coming out after five on a Friday to help a seagull. They didn't believe me of course, but time proved me right.

After finishing our meal, my friend and I sat for a while enjoying the sea and when it was time to go I picked up the gull in my coat and returned to my car. The parking booth attendant looked at Macawber wryly, no doubt thinking to himself that we were mad tourists, but said nothing.

The next day I took Macawber to my vet.

The guess was that he had botulism- picked up from eating garbage, and common for sea town seagulls. I brought Macawber back home and installed him in the second bathroom where he stayed for a couple of weeks until he was eating normally and exercising in the bath. Eventually I took him back to my vet- who is very patient with me-

and we placed Macawber in their outside courtyard so that they could watch him and see whether he could fly.

By the afternoon he had flown up and over the rooftops and back to his life.

Seagulls and the cries they make bring back for many of us the memories of seaside walks, afternoons on the beach, days on the water, and crisp Autumnal afternoons under a pale grey sky on busy farms.

They are the iconic seaside postcard, the symbol of freedom through flight thanks to RS Bach, and as pervasive as our own species.

They have the audacity to challenge us, to impose their demands upon us as they dive bomb our take away meals and snatch food from our unprepared fingers. Their very human-like adaptability may well cost them their existence as humans do not take kindly to competition.

Until then however, the sound of them greeting the sunrise evokes the nostalgic warmth of childhood, and the clandestine habits used to feed them when no one is watching.

Day 72- Books

There are people who read, and then there are book people! LOL

All my life, books have been an integral part of my days, an eclectic assortment of genres and memories.

When I was living in Jordan, my daughter thoughtfully bought me a Kindle so that I didn't have to carry weighty tomes across national borders in my suitcase-

Sadly the Kindle didn't survive the Ukraine, but that's another story.

And while I appreciated the gesture, reading for pleasure off a tablet has never appealed to me.

I like the physicality of books-

The feel of them in my hands, the texture of the paper under my fingertips, the size of them as I turn them over to read the outside covers, the look of them on my shelves- and anywhere else I can stash them.

Tablets are utilitarian, allowing the reader to enlarge the text to an easily readable size when our optic nerves start to seize up, but books... books are now of another time, they hide their treasures deep within their folds, and make you work to find them.

There is an awesome beauty to the oldest of books, as one gazes at yellowed parchment or vellum, stands humbled by the handwritten words and illustrated manuscripts, smells the mustiness of centuries as you gently ease open the cracked leather bindings....

Modern digital books can't hope to capture the heart and the very soul in the same way. It's like comparing apples and oranges-

We all enjoy the fruit, but the flavours just aren't the same.

Books, regardless of the stories they contain, have an independent value in their own right to book lovers- perhaps because they conjure up nostalgia for a time when our pace was slower, when young men and women could sit quietly and ponder without feeling that they were wasting time.

And perhaps it's because books just make a house look lived in- and for the same reason.

Day 73- Catnaps

Catnaps were renamed Power Naps in Thatcher's era, but it's catnaps still for me.

My father introduced me to the concept while I was at uni, and it was just as well since I had some very eccentric sleeping patterns- mainly involving all night discussions that might change our world. Ah the idealism of Youth.

How relevant now.

I still rely on catnaps, happily allowing myself the joy of sleeping when I feel tired, knowing that when I wake up I will feel the better for it- as long as my total sleep time is fairly constant at five to six hours. Or maybe eight. Or is it ten?

Who knows?!

The trick is to switch off completely and snooze intensely, just like a cat, and wake up primed for activity.

It's a powerful way to Be.

Day 74- Radio 3

I recently have had to change my car, and one of the eccentricities of the newer one is that the radio doesn't want me to tune in to my local channel effectively. The sound of static can be quite irritating, so I ended up listening to Radio Three this morning on my way into work.

The opening duet from The Marriage of Figaro took me back to the first LP's my mother gave me- Peter and the Wolf, Grieg's piano concerto in A minor, Tchaikovsky's violin concerto in D, Figaro and West Side Story.

I was not yet ten.

The early introduction to opera served me well when several decades later I was hired by the regional daily newspaper- the Western Morning News- to be their ballet and opera critic.

After Figaro, one of Vivaldi's long undiscovered flute concertos came on the air, and made me think of how Justine was a natural flautist from childhood- I had played the violin, and both of us stopped when we went to university. I keep telling Justine that she can always return to it in later years. Not so me- I had to sell my instrument when my ex-husband refused to pay for a medical procedure before we were married- I actually fainted in the Tate after handing the violin over. Such drama.

Then Radio Three played some choral music, and I was transported to Truro Cathedral where as one of a Thousand Voices I sang The Messiah at Christmas. Fabulous.

Radio Three....

I wonder how many teenagers even know it exists, much more listen to it?!

Do they listen to classical music at all, I wonder?

It doesn't matter either way I suppose, but I'm deeply grateful that my mother saw fit to "educate" me, as she put it, because there is something sublime in listening to music that stirs the mind and soul.

Day 75- Armistice

Blessed are the Peacemakers:
    For they shall be called the Children of God.

Day 76- Fallibility

So today I completely messed up.

Work family meeting and hadn't insured one of the family received the invite. Totally my fault, and necessitated having to cancel the meeting.

I feel so annoyed with myself at making such a rookie mistake.

So- being fallible reminds us that we aren't fool proof, that there are times when we screw up, make a misstep or the wrong decision.

It reminds us to be humble and more accommodating of others' failures.

And being fallible allows us to offer others the opportunity to be that way towards us- to show forgiveness, understanding, compassion and tolerance. To behave with Grace.

And that's no small gift for us to give.

Making mistakes teaches us the need for humility, the acceptance of failure and the resolution to make things better.

To err is Human, to forgive Divine...

And by not being perfect we can touch upon the divinity within all of us.

Ironically, the now rescheduled family meeting looks as if it will be a far better one than the one I've had to cancel.

Day 77 – Predictability

Earlier today I saw an advert for a film called Ordinary Love-

I knew what was meant but the title jarred with me a bit because there's nothing ordinary about love (which I'm guessing the film goes on to prove.)

Love is amazing, enduring, passionate, tolerant, sacrificing, enduring, intoxicating, resolute, patient... and so much much more.

The term "ordinary" is often used as a pejorative, as in not quite good enough, or special enough- run of the mill, commonplace, predictable.

Most days upon getting to the office space I often use at County Hall, I turn on the overhead lights and open the window. My manager once said to me, "You're so predictable," to which I replied, "I like to be be predictable, it gives people a false sense of security."

Knowing someone is predictable allows us the gift of feeling secure, of feeing safe- we are able to trust how that person will respond or react to situations, to us, and so we feel able to relax and trust the relationship . It enables the letting down of personal barriers and the possibility of honesty across the board.

So I'm happy to be predictable, to be ordinary in that sense, because I want the people who love me to be able to feel secure that they know me deeply enough to trust me.

And yet, one has to acknowledge, that what is ordinary for one person will not be ordinary for another, and that is what makes everything so totally UNpredictable.

Day 78- Rest

It's been a trying week, and it's only Wednesday! Nothing personal, just work related, and I can't claim to be without fault- so quite weary.

Love coming back to my cottage though, and having the freedom to do precisely as I wish.

Even though I believe we all have that freedom, and am aware of how controversial a statement that is, I am grateful for my own.

It's a blessing.

Day 79- Conversation

As Stephen Hawkins said,

Just keep talking.

Conversation.

In our days of internet connections, it's become much easier to speak with the people we wish to communicate with, all around the world. A long long way from the crackled half heard phone lines from decades ago that allowed family, lovers and friends to hear the voices of those held precious by heart and soul.

Back in the 1960's, when we still dialled numbers in red phone boxes or waited for operators to connect us long distance, my grandmother would wait patiently for a chance to phone her beloved at Whitehall. He worked for the MOD and was always muttering sotto voce about amber alerts and security risks.

Nana was allowed only to use the phone on the Embankment and had strict instructions around what she was and was not permitted to talk about- all the lines were tapped you see.

So Nana would hold fast to her sixpence or shilling and brave any weather in order to tell George that she loved him and hoped to see him later that afternoon, then we would walk up to St. James and feed the ducks- no small feat on little legs!

Now I can simply tap my phone and hear voices from my friends anywhere in the world- the sights and sounds of Bali, Mexico, Australia, Spain, Canada, all right here next to me in a nanosecond- and I can talk for hours on end to dear friends that live in those places, the distances between us shrinking to the width of an iPhone in the comfort of my living-room.

Ironically, as sharing our voices has become easier, most people choose to send texts instead- the sheer bother of actually having to converse and play an active thinking role in a two way shared communication far too onerous when you can dash off a text in shorthand, add an emoticon and go on your way. Texts are however, easy prey for misinterpretation, as vocal nuance and subtlety cannot be matched by two dimensional words.

So I'm grateful, grateful that in my time I have the extravagance of easy conversations, easy connections, constantly, just to keep talking.

Day 80-Pyjamas

Coming home and changing into loose comfortable clothes and just doing as much or as little as you wish to do.

Pyjamas- bliss.

Living here in Brigadoon, it's not unknown for me to put on my dressing gown first thing in the morning and take the hounds out for a wee opposite the cottage- nor am I the only one!! My eighty-four year old neighbour also nips out in her dressing gown at first light with her JRT.

My mother, living with me in one of my colder lets, used to simply tuck her winter nightie into her trousers and keep it on all day just to keep warm- we used to laugh at how totally unerotic the effect was.

These days I'm more fortunate, and I can relax in PJs just to be comfortable and not to be warm. It's a really relaxed way to finish a day.

Day 81- Dogs

Growing up in Liberia, I didn't have a family dog as such- there were many strays and my parents used to feed some, but when I was about seven my parents took in a back and white pup and called him White Paws.

As a child in Guyana, my mother's family had been too pragmatic to have a house pet, but she was a loving and caring soul and so she doted on White Paws. He looked like a Border Collie, I can still see him, but he was killed by a passing driver before he grew into an adult, and we didn't have any more pet dogs after that.

In fact, now that I think about it, my parents never did have a dog again- we had cats, one of which even had her kittens in my mother's office desk, and sometimes several at once, but never another dog. It wasn't until I married that dogs became a part of my life- and I was born in their year.

Champers was my first, a golden ball of fluff, American Cocker, that sadly took a dislike to little people after my husband kicked her under the table- I suppose she felt that children were the only thing she could dominate. Still, she was my psychic shadow, knew my every thought, and kept my father company during his last days- sitting beside him listening to Radio 4 and howling for a fortnight at exactly the time he died in the wee hours of the morning.

Other than the Yankees, as they are called, Borzoi's have always been my breed of choice. Romantic illusions to be sure of myself on galloping horses accompanied by these tall, graceful beasts cavorting through the countryside. And I've managed to always have at least one since my first, Rimsky, in the early eighties.

Borzois are head-turners, if for no other reason but for their size, and I'm grateful that one has never won outright at Crufts, since the breed standard is still fairly pure.

The breed introduced me to my son's godparents- benched next to us at shows.John- of Star Wars, Bond and many other films fame, was one of the gentlest souls I have ever met. He died far far too young, and the movie industry lost one of their shining lights.

My husband was a St. Bernard man, and so we had a small pack of them at Fairseat- two of the bitches rescued from a puppy farm in Dobwalls. The owner had dogs incarcerated everywhere and fed them on boiled tripe- the smell was horrendous- and so we ended up not just buying a puppy (these were the days long before we even knew what puppy farms were) who was the most fantastic old fashioned St. Bernard- meaning she looked more like a leonburger- that we named Sheba, but also took away a six year old girl called Heidi who was very much the worse for wear. Heidi had the gentlest nature, and lived with us for several years afterwards, having one more litter.

Sheba was extremely athletic and would easily climb up Roughtor and leap over styles. She lived to fifteen and died in my arms on the kitchen floor in front of the wood burner.

At our peak, we had nine St. Bernards, and when we'd roll up onto Polzeath beach in the winter in the Range Rover and open the boot, they would all leap out and run into the surf- it was a glorious sight. I had them trained so that I could walk them all together as a pack on leads, which was also quite a sight!!

When I left Cornwall, I brought Champers with me, and the children asked for a Jack Russel puppy......... Their father naturally obliged by buying a puppy for Grant, Pickle, and Justine had a retired bitch called Vimto. I must have been a very bad person in a previous life!! I have NEVER wanted a Jack Russel- ever. Ha ha.

MJ is Pickle's daughter and now fourteen, and snuffles her way around the cottage constantly as her sight is failing. She has pancreatitis and needs a very expensive diet to maintain her. My Ex has definitely had the loudest laugh.

I am also home to Emma, another breed I never wanted- labradors-but here I am with one. Emma is a wonderful old-fashioned stamp of Labrador, low centre of gravity, good limbs, fantastic temperament unless she's on guard, and with a really noble head and expressive eye. Not like so many of the newer labs, that have heads which look more like skulls, with small beady eyes and a slightly manic expression...I wonder which breeder decided that was an improvement to our noble gun-dogs so popular in the English countryside?

Dogs hold a special place in the English psyche. They have been an integral part of our lives for centuries- loved, cosseted, adored, spoilt, surrogate children, and also abandoned, mistreated, abused, starved, neglected and killed.... surrogate children.

We choose to often forget that they are intrinsically pack animals, and hunting carnivores at that, and so condemn them to houses in solitary confinement, over feed them on treats and carbohydrates, and dress them in outfits that not even surrogate children would want to wear.

No small wonder that so many dogs in our world now have behavioural issues, skin conditions, and a plethora of medical problems.... like our children.

Dogs are amazing creatures, and like so many of our animal companions, forgive us many of our short comings and trespasses. They give us unquestioning loyalty, unconditional love, constant companionship, protection if needed and inspirational honesty.

They allow me to walk unafraid at the darkest of times in the most isolated of places without a second thought.

They welcome me home when I return and tolerate my absence while I am gone.

They fit around my choices of life style and welcome my friends and a whole caravanserai of other animals.

They adapt to whatever living conditions I provide and accompany me on any travel I demand of them.

Dogs give my life positive energy, spreading love in every room.

Emma is snoring, MJ is curled up next to her, and Ellisar lies stretched full length on the kitchen carpet with one of the kittens playing hide and seek in his belly hair... it's a magical scene of harmony and contentment.

My Year of the Dog may come round only once every twelve years, but sharing my life with dogs has become a full time experience, and I can hear my mother's laugh and my father's voice as they watch the Bernies frolic in the surf.

Day 82- Boundaries

In my line of work, we are always carping on about boundaries- and how necessary they are for the successful parenting of children. We advise parents that they need to be adults and provide boundaries within which their children can learn to explore and develop safely. We encourage parents to be consistent and allow their children to push against boundaries if necessary, because it is only in finding resistance that growing children can learn about where their safety lies, and this makes them feel secure and, ultimately, loved and cared for. Children need boundaries, and adults have to not only recognise this but also have the confidence to maintain the status quo when challenged by a toddler full of teenage angst and rebellion.

We have loads of boundaries in this country. They date back centuries, and we never did have our social revolution.

Social boundaries probably rank uppermost, and can really be noticed playing their subtle part as the insidious feudal nature of our society shows itself around a political happening.

We still doff our caps to the pin-stripe wearing Etonian vocal patterns with the blind reverence of the peasant workers who tilled the fields several hundred years ago. We still talk about a class system, and take pride in the social customs that relegate the working man in the street to a disadvantaged second best.

Then there is the boundary of inverted snobbery that revels in a working class past- there's that reference again- where the chip on the shoulder slags off any and every one who speaks properly - as in from the South- and knows their grammar.

Then we have economic boundaries. The haves and the have nots. Those who want everything without wanting to sacrifice anything for it.

Once inexorably linked to class and inherited wealth- God forbid you came from "rich Trade"- the nouveau riche (also a demeaning term- there's that old class structure again) were looked down upon by their snooty aristocratic neighbours while the wealthy didn't even bother to dirty their hands.

And so it became acceptable to strive to have everything but to not earn it oneself- and that's part of our social culture now.

Only it's spread, trickled down the hierarchy and permeated every rung of the social ladder. (Yet another metaphor based on its better to be at the top.)

When did it become acceptable to have numerous children when one can't afford to raise even one without using money provided by other hard working people? And when I say numerous, I don't mean two or three, I mean eight or nine.

The aristocracy has done it for ages, but they could afford to. Most cannot.

When did it become acceptable to have all the modern conveniences but not have to inconvenience yourself at all in order to have them. And I'm not talking pots and pans, I'm talking smart phones and apple televisions. And yes, I know now that everything is done online, benefit claimants need internet access. Well, libraries have pc's available to all. No, wait, we now don't have libraries either.

In this country we have a massive burden brought about by hundreds of years of social boundaries that we like to honour but that no longer serve. The working class is now the bourgeoisie, even though our political parties still use the labels Labour and Tory, when there is really nothing so clear cut about them.

It's all rather tedious and preciously short-sighted.

We are wasting Time.

We are of one Earth and we are faffing around emphasising our differences, reinforcing our boundaries, when we should be breaking them down.

We should be running hell for leather into one another's arms and joining hands in what might well be the one last ditch attempt to save Humanity on this earth.

Instead, we rattle on about race, and colour, and creed, about nationalism and past glories, and fail to accept or even recognise our current failings- and we are failing, ourselves, and one another. Our world.

Boundaries.

Children need boundaries.

Adults should not. Adults should know how to behave, how to regulate their behaviour and their responses while living in a social framework- No man is an island after all (Educated reference to John Donne, metaphysical poet. And now I'm being satirical. In joke- Donne the satirist.)

It's time that we grew up, grasped the responsibility of our choices and owned them, and stopped bleating on about how difficult things are unless everything is provided for us.

We are not infants, and it's time we stopped accepting social mores that treat us as such.

It's time we stopped tugging our forelocks in deferential myopia and started asking the questions that really matter- how are we going to change this entrenched paradigm that disadvantages millions of people around the globe?

Do we want to live or don't we?

Boundaries- when you are an adult, you create your own.

Day 83- Unicorns

This past weekend my granddaughter came to spend the day with me. While in the car she asked, "Unicorns don't live in the world anymore, do they Nana- but they used to, didn't they? In olden days? Why aren't there any unicorns now? Where have they all gone?"

Most people with experience with young children- my granddaughter is five- will understand when I say that my mind was reeling with trying to find the best way to answer- at the same time being truthful while not destroying the magic of a child's imagination.

"No, unicorns aren't around anymore.....not like they were in olden times....."

"But where have they all gone? Why did they go away?"

Panic starting to set in now as I switch gear and start multi-tasking- radio three playing Andre Previn's Song on violin- damn the headlight still isn't working properly- where does the woman with the second hand rug live- must dig up some compost on the yard for the blue spruce I want to repot- is Mole Valley open on Sunday- where are the unicorns now??

"The unicorns all went away to live in a special place...."

"Why?"

A million synapses firing as I search for an answer of hope and wisdom...

"Well....when unicorns lived some of the people started to be unkind to one another and that made the unicorns very sad, so they decided to go and live in a special unicorn place."

"What's it like?"

"What do you think it would be like, a special place where unicorns live?"

Slam dunk! Goal! I can now relax and listen to the wisdom of a child.

"It'd have trees with candy canes on, and gingerbread houses (hang on, I'm thinking, aren't we mixing up our metaphors here?) and flowers made of cupcakes....(cupcakes? Where did those come from?).... and rainbow grass."

What?!?

"What's rainbow grass?"

"Rainbow grass is when a unicorn touches the grass with his horn (HIS horn?? Why a male unicorn?) and the grass changes to all the colours of the rainbow. Then you can eat it and it makes you never be sick. It's magic."

Just like that. It's magic.

When my granddaughter was a toddler, I would put her to bed and invent a story about two unicorns who had adventures. It never failed to settle her and I would say as I left her room, "Dream about unicorns Darling."

Unicorns... what is it about them that so grabs our imagination, that allows us to welcome them into our lives and surround ourselves with pictures, tapestries, toys, clothes and school bags with friendly unicorn faces that have rainbows plaited into their manes? This ethereal mythical creature, symbol of purity and grace, with a horn able to heal sickness, is now commonplace in children's lives...and that can't be a bad thing.

As I walked home tonight I looked up at the clouds and for just a second a shooting star shot across a patch of bare sky. I automatically made a wish, connecting with all of my hopes and dreams and deep beliefs that there is magic in the world.

Unicorns bring to us a sense of wonder, a hope for joy and delight, a wish for magic to once again fill our senses and make our world a better place.

It's a worthwhile dream.

Day 84- Salt

Yesterday I woke up with one of those dagger in the throat sore throats, and I immediately knew I must gargle with salt- last night the pain had gone.

Salt gets a lot of bad press these days, but it is an amazing compound- sodium and chlorine- NaCl- and vital for optimum body physiology.

It is the main source of sodium and chloride ions in the human diet. Sodium is essential for nerve and muscle function and is involved in the regulation of fluids in the body. Chloride ions serve as important electrolytes by regulating blood pH and pressure.

On a more mundane level, salt is a great cleanser, preserved and melter of ice!

Intriguingly, salt has also become an integral part of the archane arts, it's crystals used as protection again dark forces, while the Romans often paid their soldiers in salt because it was such a valuable resource.

Today we are spoilt. We take salt for granted and are very wasteful of it. We no longer spend lifetimes mining it or transporting it, and we are spoilt with choices-

Himalayan, Sea, iodised ....

For me, I'm grateful for its healing properties and for its culinary uses- and that it keeps my neural network firing.

Day 86- Reunions

Weddings and funerals, the saying goes, brings families and friends together- often after years of not seeing one another. The phrase is usually spoken with a sense of irony, particularly when it juxtaposes the sadness of a funeral with the pleasure of catching up with long-lost friends or family members.

Today was such a day for me, as I shared a day with dear old friends that I haven't seen for a while while at the same time saying farewell to their elderly relative.

Reunions are special. They bring people together, and allow them to share cherished memories and treasured moments. Shared dreams, shared experiences, shared adventures, laughter and love.

Reunions allow time to drop away, and create opportunities for friends to come together as if no time has passed at all, so that the past is again the present and all things are possible.

When you've enjoyed as many special friendships as I have, reunions are a true gift, and I'm always grateful when life gives me the opportunity to once again touch base with individuals no longer in my day to day life.

Today was one of those days.

Day 87- Advent

When I was away at boarding school, my mother used to say that Christmas didn't start until I returned home for the holidays. I've come to understand what she meant.

Unlike my mother, who had my father to share celebrations with, I no longer have a partner and as such most of my sharing centres around my children and their families- but I know many people who live by themselves and don't have extended family to share Christmas with.

I enjoy Christmas, always have, and have little time for the bah humbugs of this world who tar the celebrations with the disdain of cynicism and criticise the commercialism which surrounds all of our cultural holidays... we don't have to buy into it- pun intended- if we do not want to.

This year I am spending Christmas with Justine, and so I couldn't decide whether to put up my decorations or not... what was the point when the house would be standing empty...? Also, I knew that once I started, bringing forth memories and ornaments that all have a story attached, that I wouldn't be able to stop!

Which is exactly what's happened.

This afternoon I decided to make the wreath, a little less flamboyant than my norm as the door is quite small- ha ha- and then I started delving into the decorations box.

It's been fun.

I wish I was going to share the Santa's and reindeer and lights with others but the kittens are having great fun pouncing on a long string of green beads, and the twinkling lights on my broomstick outside seem to have developed a mind of their own

It's very odd.

Advent is the first season of the Church Year, the four Sundays leading up to the birth of Christ as celebrated within the Christian faith-

It is a time of preparation, of expectation, a period of anticipation that culminates in the great joy of Christ's birth.

And that should be cause for great happiness, whether we are at one with our friends and families, or with our Selves.

Day 85- Energy

My grandmother used to say,

All Energy comes from Divine Source, and the Divine is infinite, so there can never be a lack of energy within ourselves, as long as we maintain our connection to the Divine.

Nana spoke in language now commonplace, but when I first heard these words I was a small child, and she was paraphrasing Mary Baker Eddy of Christian Science fame.

Energy.

Now we are told- and I believe- that everything IS energy, we all simply perceive that All from our own frequency of vibration.

As the organised religions of the world have become increasingly more mundane and less and less spiritual, people have lost their intrinsic link to their gods, and more and more attached to their material world. It is not a change that has served us well.

This era is being heralded by many as the Time for Change- the New

Age- the great Awakening...

We can but hope.

As each and every individual battles with the dark and sticky problems of their worldly lives, it's hard to connect to the unbearable light-ness of Be-ing (thank you Milan Kundera) but each and every time we do- whether by a sunrise, a child's laugh, a salty breeze or a lark's song- we raise our own Energy and thus the energy of the world around us.

We all need to find our link to what my grandmother called the Divine Source-

And hang onto it tightly in the battles ahead.

Day 88- Ingenuity

Travelling and living in what are referred to as Third World Countries hones the mind and the imagination, it makes you have to think outside the box of habit and conformity, and leads to powers of invention and creative thinking.

Like the shower made from a can punched with a screwdriver, the camel dung used to plug a leaking Land Rover radiator and the famous broken fan belt replacement- silk stockings.

I was listening yesterday morning to the surgeon David Nott as he remembered his time on the frontlines and recounted a C-section he'd performed in Chad. The mother of seven died from an internal haemorrhage, and when he later went to check up on her children, they had all disappeared.

It reminded me of a story my father told from his cycling safari across Africa.

When he and his travel companion reached the Congo, they encountered a man and his wife deep in the forest who were working with the Congo Pygmies on the Epulu River. They ran Camp Putnam and later Anne wrote a book about their time there.

The night my father would talk about took place in the very basic medical clinic that the Putnams ran for the local people. The clinic was in the middle of the bush and had neither electricity nor surgical equipment.

A native woman had arrived late at night with three or four other women. She was obviously in an advanced state of pregnancy, and very ill.

Pat, who was in a wheelchair, gave her an internal exam and realised immediately that the baby had died and needed to be removed as quickly as possible.

Ann urged him not to touch the woman as her possible death could bring a wealth of local bad feeling with it, and the Putnams were extremely isolated and vulnerable.

Pat was not deterred.

Giving orders that someone should hold the lantern- a kerosine lamp- and with my father squinting trying to take notes, Pat proceeded to deliver the stillborn child.

He used two large serving spoons.

His patient survived the procedure.

In the morning, when Pat went to check on her, the woman had returned to the forest.

Day 89- Air Ambulances

In the wee hours of this morning the weather outside was having a great fandango, and I thought how happy I was to be inside.

Earlier on, as night started to settle, I drove home listening to the sound of a helicopter, and watched it as it headed out to the coast, searchlights scanning the ground. I don't know if that particular chopper was looking for felons or lost souls, but I do know how astounded I have always been that the emergency air ambulance services have only very recently become partly government funded, as opposed to not government funded at all.

Living on the coast, in a county where many villages are set off the beaten track, having an air ambulance is a Godsend- and they do save lives. In all weathers. Long may they continue to do so.

Day 90- Birthdays

Today is my children's father's birthday- he would have been ninety-six years old were he still in this evolution.

Birthdays of those no longer with us tend to make me reflect upon who that person was to me, how I perceived them, the ways in which we related to one another and the impact we had upon each other's lives.

He had a massive impact upon mine.

Birthdays are a chance to celebrate, to rejoice in shared moments, close friendships and loving family- to give thanks for someone special to our lives.

I never saw any pictures of my Ex's childhood, or any of crazy parties in his teens or early years- I do have some from his seventieth though, when I had invitations printed and sent out to seventy guests- it was quite a night and Fairseat was alight with glamour and bling.

Birthdays remind us that we have successfully completed yet another journey around our Sun- a journey that gives us opportunities to live and to learn about both ourselves and one another- not all the Lessons are happy or welcomed, but each one is surely relevant to the person we grow into being...

Which is why birthdays are to be treasured and enjoyed... hopefully with lots of cake and something bubbly to drink.

Day 91 - Walks

It's almost two in the morning and I've just come in from walking the hounds down to the beach. Full moonlit sky and frost on the ground- quiet beautiful time of night which I can enjoy thanks to a impromptu nap earlier this evening... I knew it would be a perfect night for a late jaunt with the dogs to the sea.

I've always loved walking- but not the gadget laden hi tech walking so popular now, I'm more of a Middle Ages type of walker- strolling along in sandals with a bag slung over my shoulder and just enough money to see me to my destination.

I walk from the hip, unlike many women who move from the knee, and so cover more distance with each stride- my "boarding school stride" as my father used to call it.

I fantasise about walking the Camino- and dawdling along it as other more intense hikers follow it gung ho from stamp to stamp, and now also the West Highland Way- although I fear my natural hermit personality is put off by the thought of sharing Nature with many other enthusiasts!

Best for me then to wander in the quiet of the night, enjoying the solitude and the calm after the hustle and chaos of a working day- and I'm grateful that I can do that. Venture out into the darkness unfettered and unafraid- and just breathe.

Day 92- Good Health

As the spectre of increased privatisation spreads outwards with the oncoming dawn, I am increasingly thankful for my knowledge of homeopathy, herbal lore, nutrition and alternative therapies.

Now in my sixties, I am blessed with good health and the ability to self-medicate with efficacy whenever I feel unwell... hopefully I will never need surgical procedures, as I certainly could not afford to pay for even the tiniest operation through private health care.

For those individuals who do not have private pensions- or access to those of their partners, private trust funds- or access to one, or are earning enough money to be in the top tax bracket, middle to old age can be daunting when joined to ill health, chronic medical conditions, mental health issues or all of the above.

There is much coverage currently about having to choose between heating and eating, but for many older individuals the choice will soon be between food and medicine.

Winter has come.

Day 93- Sleep

I am one of the lucky people who can not only catnap, but can also fall asleep instantly and sleep anywhere.

This has served me well when travelling, when I've had to sleep in a variety of positions on a variety of materials!

When I visited Nana with my parents I would sleep on an ancient leather two seater couch only long enough to accommodate my upper body- my lower body was supported by two dining chairs positioned at right angles to the couch.

Years later I ended up sleeping in a cast iron bathtub to escape my mother's ceaseless snoring.

I've slept on many floors, on bare earth and concrete, and balanced precariously on my side along a plank barely eight inches wide- some subconscious awareness kept me very still!

To sleep, perchance to dream.....

Sadly, I recall very few dreams, but I can only hope that I do some of my best work while sound asleep.

My favourite snoozes though are those with my animal companions asleep around me, or with my grandchildren nestled in my arms as once my children were.

As their rhythmic breathing reflects an internal calm, it is easy to put aside the daily conflicts and enjoy instead the peace of the just.

Day 94- Faith

Faith is the ability to suspend a need for empirical evidence and believe- the KNOWING of something regardless of being able to evidence it in tangible form.

Today is Sunday, and around the world many millions of people will be attending religious services to honour a god or goddess that they believe in.

Sadly, many of those millions no longer remember exactly what those deities represent for humanity, and instead only follow the rituals of their religions having forgotten the essence behind the faith.

On a more mundane level- in as of the world (mundo)- we all place our faith in people at some time.

As a newborn child, we have faith that our hunger will be removed by our mothers, as children that we will be kept safe by our parents, as adults that those we love will not cause us suffering.

And when that faith is proved to be wrong, the damage done to our deep psyche is profound and far-reaching.

And very seldom healed.

Faith allows us to Hope against the odds, and Hope gives us Trust- that life will evolve in its own time into what is best for us in the long run...

Are we all sages, or simple fools...?

For my part, I wish everyone could reconnect to the faith deep within their souls that is born of love, the Love that underpins all the teachings of all the religions of all the people of all the world.

I wish that men and women everywhere would seek out that Love within themselves and use it to reach out to others and create a world of peace and tolerance and well-being.

A world where the resounding energy is Divine in the truest sense.

Now, more than ever, we must have Faith that this shall someday be so.

Day 95- Christmas

Christmas within my family has always been a time of sharing love- whether that is manifested through gifts, time shared, effort expended or simply good food and drink!

My childhood is full of happy memories of Christmases spent with my parents and their friends- precocious only child! LOL- of celebrations with my grandmother, and of just KNOWING that Father Christmas was real.

As an adult I can remember only two less than perfect Christmas mornings, but even those were saved by the concerted efforts of all concerned to turn the day into a happy memory.

These days Christmas gets a lot of bad press, as people argue around the mass commercialism that we ourselves have allowed to evolve, but there is always choice.

Yesterday, because I shan't be in residence next week (anyone fancy a week in Brigadoon?), my son and his family came for lunch. It was a very simple meal, nothing extravagant (payday not until Friday) but it was a really lovely lovely afternoon.

The children were settled and happy, the atmosphere was relaxed, and even the animals - canine guest also arrived- were accommodating of one another!

It brought home to me the true value of the Christmas spirit-

That when people are prepared to work with one another in a loving way, inspired by a true selfless love, miracles can happen.

Back in the seventies, when I was flying backwards and forwards to Liberia, we had our first armed hijacking of an international airline.

As a result, Zurich airport was crawling with armed militia in all the terminals, and the increased security checks were causing huge queues (those were the days!) and delays.

I was carrying as hand luggage a large cardboard box filled with Christmas presents from my grandmother.

Nana used to triple wrap- tissue paper decorated with hand cut out decorations from d cards or paper, top wrap of Christmas wrapping paper and bows and tinsel, then all put together in a fitted box, wrapped and decorated again with more ribbon and tinsel- I always had strict orders to "froo froo" the ribbons before putting the presents from her under the tree. She also scented the tissue paper.

That year in Zurich the middle-aged customs lady opened the cardboard box and looked in with dismay. She took in at a glance all the beauty and love that was illustrated by the wrapping on the presents, and began to silently cry as she opened each and every one. Her remorse was heart breaking to watch, and I kept reassuring her that I understood that she had to do what she was doing to keep everyone safe.

I can still see her in my mind's eye.

Three hours late, our plane took off.

She had rewrapped every little parcel and lovingly replaced everything as it had been.

Christmas-

I know people don't all celebrate it or condone it, but the core values behind it are vital to our humanity and once a year, everyone is able to buy into those values, some way or another, if they so wish.

I do.

Day 96- Flowers

Just thinking about flowers makes me want to smile.

Sometime ago, and I really don't know how, sunflowers became synonymous with me in my friends' and family's mind- such a delight. And I do love them, with their bright almost gaudy faces, turning to face the sun as it journeys across the sky.

Roses too, and scented lilies, are among my favourites, and it gives me genuine delight when they bloom for me throughout the summer on whatever outside space I am attached to.

With time, I have come to appreciate that flowers are happiest left unpicked, but I do enjoy cut flowers indoors even so- and happily choose flowers over other extravagances.

And now I muse on the philosophical conundrum- does a rose bloom that goes unseen...? Is it only our perception of the rose that makes it real...?

On the day I was born, my father spent the time leading up to my arrival in the pub with my uncle, having been banished there by an overzealous Matron-

Those were not the days of shared birthing experiences in the delivery room.

Upon returning to the hospital, my father (undoubtedly a little merry) stopped and bought all the flowers being sold at the gates by a street vendor for my mother- a typically grand gesture for him.

I had already arrived, and no doubt thought in my newborn state that the sudden arrival of flowery scents was in my honour- no wonder I love flowers so much to this day.

Day 97-Achievement

When my children were growing up we had a conversation around the phrase, "I'm so proud of you..."

I always felt a little uncomfortable with the phrase because it transferred the achievement to me instead of allowing the person who had achieved whatever it was to own the pride for it. So instead I would say, I'm thrilled for you, or I'm so happy for you, and only when they were finally old enough to understand the subtlety of words, I'm so proud to be your mother.

It has become an in joke between Justine and myself over time, with her sometimes asking, "Are you proud of me?" And I always reply, "Very proud that you are my daughter."

Achievements are something that we all should rejoice in, particularly when those achievements help others less fortunate than ourselves- when we are able to BE the good we want to see in the world.

And the tools we use to successfully achieve our hopes and wishes are born from a multitude of circumstances, from the moment of our birth- we are lucky if the tools stack up to benefit not just ourselves but the world around us.

And I cannot deny that when I think about my two children, now both adults with children of their own, that I am totally impressed by the people they have grown into- and that being their mother ranks as one of my greatest achievements.

Day 98- Water

I've always been a water-baby, either on it, in it or under it! When in Aqaba I would spend almost entire weekends on the end of a jetty in between snorkelling and diving, and I always have to resist the desire to breathe beneath the surface.

For those of us who have travelled to less industrialised countries, being able to turn a tap and have water come out of the faucet is a real gift- to be able to drink that water safely even more so!

And now, here in Devon, we are being deluged with rainfall, the countryside water sodden to capacity, roads and fields flooded, while other countries are suffering horrendously from fires and drought.

We are so careless of our water here, squandering one of our greatest natural resources, wasting the opportunities to harvest this natural bounty and instead letting all the water drain out to sea.

Water. There will come a time when it will cost more than gold, for water sustains life, and we have already privatised water supplies in the UK. (How was that even allowed to happen?!)

Water makes up over ninety per cent of our biological physiology- and as such lends to each and every one of us it's remarkable qualities- responsible for both our physical and emotional wellbeing.

Who among us has not gratefully downed a glass of ice cold water on a hot summer's day, or curled themself around a hot cup of tea to chase away the winter's cold?

We take water for granted in this country, we run taps while we brush our teeth, flush toilets at will, water garden lawns and motor cars, hardly thinking about what our lives would be like if water were rationed, as it often is in hotter climes.

In Jordan every family was limited to one four foot cubed container per week...

Think about that.

Day 99- Love

Love..........

In all of its guises, complexity, idiosyncrasies, shapes, forms and applications...

Love is who we are and what we aspire to be,

Love IS Everything.

We ignore that at the peril of our own destruction- for we ARE Love, if we only allowed ourselves to shine.

Day 100- Life.

A Hundred Days.

It's been a worthwhile pastime, a working meditation... seeking paths to gratitude through the vagaries of existence.

Life- let's ignore that over half of it is Illusion (lie) and concentrate rather on the half that is potential possibility- IF.

And to quote Kipling-

If you can fill the unforgiving minute with sixty seconds worth of distance run,

Yours is the earth, and everything that's in it...

With all its sham, drudgery and broken dreams, it is still a beautiful world. (The Desirata)

Day 101-New Year's Eve:

My friends will know that my bedroom window overlooks my bird feeders, and this morning- as I determine to expel this ghastly flu and its symptoms - I am as per usual watching the many little birds having their morning meal. You all know how much deep joy they give to me every day.

It's the simple things.

New Year, and I'm thinking about all the blessings which fill my life every day- hence Day 101... because I want to name people in particular and say thank you.

(Since an Oscar hasn't yet come my way!)

My children of course, my son isn't on my FB link, but this year I have been deeply impressed by the man and father he has grown into being.

My daughter, who is a true Star on so many levels, and has birthed two of her own.

Rosemary and Tasha, for visiting my beloved Eunice.

Liza, my soulself in another body- really miss you.

Kryssie, my always kind and generous friend, who has reached out and helped me so many times, thank you for the birdseed!!

Tammy and Deborah, I'm SO grateful you live nearby so that I have at least one person I can go out and play with.

Lesley, my shamanic sister, who has always listened and never judged.

Lorraine and Ffyona, my fellow barefoot walkers- so much love and connection at all levels.

Catriona, my friend and soul sister, time to come home!!

My colleagues, some not on social media, who have helped and supported me through all the good times and worse times, we are an amazing team!! And the nation agrees!! LOL.

May 2020 bring David and Lorna, and others, wonderful new adventures.

Rita, Alia, Tariq, Tamara and Mark for bringing perspectives from other places.

Salutations.

ALL my horse loving friends, because I need to know I am truly insane but that insanity is a good thing!!

Tina, Natalie and Ginny- thank you for all the many times you've gone the extra mile to help me.

For Cherry, Denise, Naomi, Rochelle, Caroline, Shelley, Tracey, Hilary, Nancy, Alison, Jason, Susan- because we are always linked to our past, but these are happy links.

My amazing Amir and Philip, for travelling beside me to places few dare to tread. And always with Michail in our hearts.

For Jools and Rachel and Patricia and Levi- thank you for grabbing hold of my wing tip

AND holding on to it with Love.

Always,

Suyen

About the Author

Suyen lives in Devon with three cats, two dogs and a motley collection of house-plants and books. Her grandchildren call her Crazy Nana.

Lightning Source UK Ltd.
Milton Keynes UK
UKHW012011120123
415233UK00004B/318